Happydemic

Your Roadmap to Living and Spreading Sustainable Happiness

Larissa Redaelli

PASSIONPRENEUR
PUBLISHING

HAPPYDEMIC
Copyright © 2020 Larissa Redaelli
First published in 2020

ISBN
Print: 978-1-922456-22-9
E-book: 978-1-922456-23-6

All rights reserved. No part of this book may be reproduced, stored in a retrieval system, or transmitted by any means (electronic, mechanical, photocopying, recording, or otherwise) without written permission from the author.

Because of the dynamic nature of the Internet, any web addresses or links contained in this book may have changed since publication and may no longer be valid. The information in this book is based on the author's experiences and opinions. The views expressed in this book are solely those of the author and do not necessarily reflect the views of the publisher; the publisher hereby disclaims any responsibility for them.

The author of this book does not dispense any form of medical, legal, financial, or technical advice either directly or indirectly. The intent of the author is solely to provide information of a general nature to help you in your quest for personal development and growth. In the event you use any of the information in this book, the author and the publisher assume no responsibility for your actions. If any form of expert assistance is required, the services of a competent professional should be sought.

Publishing information
Publishing, design, and production facilitated by Passionpreneur Publishing,
A division of Passionpreneur Organisation Pty Ltd, ABN: 48640637529

www.PassionpreneurPublishing.com
Melbourne, VIC | Australia

To my life supporters and fans, my husband Alessandro, and my children Riccardo and Federico.

My family, my friends, and sixteen-year-old Camila for the book title.

To all those who have been great mentors in my career and life.

To my customers for their continuous support, loyalty, and trust.

To all the delegates that listened actively to my programmes, supported my work, believed in me, and transformed.

To all the audiences that encouraged me to keep searching, learning, and continuously improving.

To all those who have chosen my first book *Le Savoir-Vendre* out of millions of other books, decided to embrace its learnings, and have it as their new companion in their careers.

To You, Dear Reader, Dear Friend . . .

Book testimonials

Larissa has been infected with a happy DNA! Through her book *Happydemic*, she provides a well-rounded view on the topic of happiness and how to approach it.

—Moustafa Hamwi, The Passionpreneur

Few authors are able to radiate happiness, joy, and gratification through their writing like Larissa does. The world needs more people with the skills of encouragement that Larissa has.

—David G. Curmi, Executive Chairman,
Air Malta p.l.c.

I have known Larissa for more than twenty-five years now. For the longest time, Larissa has always had an interest in writing quality and compelling content. In the years I have known her, she has demonstrated exceptional competence. I have always been amazed by her passion for creativity. Larissa is intelligent, competent, dedicated, enthusiastic, honest, and has excellent communication skills, which helps her connect with everybody around her.

—Jorge Simao, Managing Director,
Eurovision Services Middle East

I met Larissa more than a decade ago in my previous employment as Chairman and CEO of a real estate group. I had invited her to deliver an introductory NLP programme to the management team. Full of positive energy, passionate, supportive, and knowledgeable, she radiated her enthusiasm to all.

—Franco Valletta, Group Chief Officer
Organisation Development and HR,
Corinthia Hotels

Larissa brings back true and simple happiness to the centre of life. I have met several life coaches, but I was rarely inspired by them as they didn't have the life experience and the inner love of others that Larissa has. Every time she faces difficulties, she addresses them with wisdom and would love others to do the same. She is an inspiring person, the European Oprah Winfrey.

—Sebastien Boucraut, Founder and Managing Partner,
Eon Partners SA

Larissa is a true inspiration, who brings good insights our way and bringing happiness to life both at a professional and a private level.

—Boubou Hallberg, CEO
SÄS Hospital Sweden

Larissa is special to me and I distinguish her from others for her determination and strength. Learning from our setbacks and celebrating our successes to then share them with others makes Larissa a Lady with a majuscule "L." As a Former Professional Soccer Player for Juventus, Verona, and other big clubs in Italy, and now as Head Soccer Coach, I teach my team to commit to results at whatever cost and never give up in front of life or sport challenges. This is what Larissa teaches us. I wish her all the luck she deserves with *Happydemic*.

—Fabrizio Cammarata, Head Soccer Coach,
Dinamo Tiranë

Larissa Redaelli's *Happydemic* is an incredible blend of her own life experience, expertise and thorough research, offering practical formulas on how to unlock your true potential and achieve your goals. Illuminating blueprint to your own pursuit of Happiness… it is so hard to put the book down.

—Biljana Halim, Marketing Specialist,
Marjan

A compelling and dynamic professional with a unique perspective and set of skills. A passion to achieve optimal results together with extensive knowledge and experience on human behaviour; Larissa is a proven catalyst for change and empowerment.

—Esmeralda Micallef Zarafa, CEO, LSF Foundation

I did not realise that thinking in a positive manner has a major effect on controlling my energy levels. You are one of those people who wants to make the day of each one of us. Your techniques in spreading positivity are the booster keys, which I learned and apply daily, mainly now to cope with COVID-19. In less than two months with you, I understood why it's really important to be emotionally strong. You made me a more powerful person. You prepared me to be a dreamer, to feel better, and to live in the first place. Thank You Very Much!

—Naema Alfalahi, Ernest Young Assistant Associate

Larissa is true to herself, no matter what; someone who goes above and beyond ordinary expectations to help someone out or even just to cheer them up. Success is the only word which describes a prosperous person like her; she is an achiever.

—Maitha Alblooshi, Emirates NBD PAL Trainee

Your Road Map Itinerary

To You	xiii
Preface	xv

☺ **The First Step** — 3

Behavioural, Cognitive, Holistic and Spiritual Approaches to Living and THEN Spreading Sustainable Happiness — 3

My Person Initiation	3
Happiness Definitions:	13
- Happiness in Philosophy	14
- Happiness in Psychology	16
- Happiness in Religions	18
- Happiness in Nations	21
- Maslow's Hierarchy of Needs	24
Happiness Measurement	25
My Definition of Happiness	26

☺ **The Second Step** — 31

Turning the Soil — 31

Depression:	33
- Depression Risk Factors	35
- How to Diagnose Depression?	36
- How is Depression Treated?	37
- Medication	38
- Psychotherapy Approach	39
- Cognitive Behavioural Therapy (CBT)	39

- Electroconvulsive Therapy (ECT)   39
- Self-Therapy   39

How My Depression Got Treated at First   40

Medication   40

Happiness Chemicals   48

Alternative Medicine Practices: 58
- Energy Medicines (Biofield Therapy, Reiki, Homoeopathy, Traditional Chinese Medicine, Ayurveda)   59
- Head and Body Massages   68
- Goodbye Toxins   75
- Mindfulness and Meditation   78

Self-Therapy   81

My Immune MNMS Detox Formula©   **85**

MIND (Mental Detox)   **86**
- Self Determination Theory: Six theories   86
- Neuroscience   88
- Positive Thinking   90
- Neuro-Linguistic Programming   92
  - NLP Definition   97
  - NLP Brief History   99
  - NLP Benefits in Business   100
  - Additional NLP Benefits   103
  - Mindset and Behaviour   105
  - The Wheel of Life   112
  - My Breakthrough Area   113

- Mind Management and Mind-Body Connection 117
- NLP Change Model 119
- Thinking Process and Information Filtering System 124
- Your Internal Filters and Thinking Map 129
- Empowering Change 158
- Cognitive Behavioural Therapy 162
  - Expectations: The Beauty and the Beast 163
- Faradarmani 173
- The Power of Now by Eckhart Tolle 176

Emotional Detox 187
- Positive Psychology and Emotional Management "PERMA" 187
- Dialectical Behaviour Therapy: 189
  - Resilience Pillars and Technique 190
  - Few Tips to Strengthen Your Resilience 191
- Emotional Intelligence and EI Model Tools To Regulate Your Emotions: "My Quick Fix List" 193
- The Secret by Rhonda Byrne 205
  - The Ten Secrets That Helped Me Transform 211

Environmental Detox 212

NUTRITION 217
- A-Z Essential Nutrients: Vitamins benefits 220
- Nutrient Promoters and Adversaries 223
- Minerals and Their Benefits 225
- Minerals Promoters and Adversaries 227
- Essential Oils and Their Benefits 229
- Essential Oils Promoters and Adversaries 229
- Fibre: The Zero-Calorie Carbohydrate 230

- Best Antioxidant Foods and ORAC Rankings — 233
- Phytochemicals and Their Benefits — 235

MOVEMENT — 240

SLEEP — 242

The Third Step — 245

Design Your Future, Architect your Roadmap — 245
S.M.A.R.T.E.R Goal-Setting Technique — 245
GROW Model — 248

The Book In One Page — 251

Crash Wake-Up Call — 253

References — 257

More about the Author — 259

Introduction to Le Savoir-Vendre — 263

With My *Happydemic* Success Wishes — 265

To You

Why Have You Chosen This book?

Have you been attracted by its title? Are you looking to improve the way you interact with the world? Are you in a challenging moment, where you don't know if you are in the right place, career, or path? Are you exhausted, stressed, or unhappy in your career and life? Are you in search of HAPPINESS? Are you in pain? Are you looking for mental clarity and inner freedom? Do you want to find the right balance and equilibrium cruise speed to fly? Are you searching for some answers to recurrent questions in today's tough and competitive world?

Happydemic, *Your Roadmap to Living and Spreading Sustainable Happiness* is your answer and your companion for your journey of change, and ultimately, a friend forever. More than a reader's history and another book, this is THE meeting of two destinies, an existential appointment in the "be" and "do" fields. You chose to buy this life manual and now your choice to take in the learnings and apply them in your day-to-day life will determine your smart and fast approach to happiness. You will have to play to win and rise stronger. You will achieve sustainable happiness only if you COMMIT to do whatever it takes; be willing to bring about awareness, courage, determination, perseverance, and consistency.

This book aims to respond to your needs by giving you personally tested best practices that you can immediately implement in your career and life on one condition, which is to **INVEST UNCONDITIONALLY**.

Are you ready for this TRUE happiness sustainable adventure?

Open the first page.

Preface

My Journey to Living and Spreading Sustainable Happiness

I published my first interactive book in French, *Le Savoir-Vendre (The Selling Know-How, 2012)*. It focuses on the technical and psychological approaches needed in the sales world using different neuroscience to embed a long-term deep rapport. It sums up over twenty years of experience in a straightforward way with seven sales steps that I created following trials, successes, and errors in my sales career. Most of our learning comes from experiences that no university can teach. I can't express the immense happiness I felt when I saw my book cover page coming out of the printing press. It took me years to decide to write about my personal experience in sales and customer relationship management, and in corporate training and vocational hospitality education (Sales and Communication Professor at the Geneva Hotel Management School).

I never thought that I would write a book one day or even be a professor or business life coach. My father is a great writer and a professor of French literature. Is it hereditary? Maybe. One thing is sure, my purpose in life, which I discovered in my late thirties, is to give and share with a larger number of people my operational and personal experiences (positive and negative); in addition to the knowledge and tips for success that I preach, teach, and apply, to allow people to excel and be happy in whatever they do.

We are all human beings walking around and spreading information about our experiences, both positive and negative. The question here is, can we become attentive and aware of the results we produce around us? Are we producing gardens that are, in turn, giving healthy fruits, colourful flowers, plants, and trees, or devastated and thirsty lands with dead plants, unhealthy flowers, and broken trees?

It is so much easier to look at the neighbour's garden than our own. I feel so grateful to have finally embraced the harvest of my own garden in and out, and I will be sharing with you my journey in cultivating resilience and building a winner's mindset and attitude towards happiness and soul salvation.

Swiss-Lebanese born, I grew up in Lebanon, a beautiful country with a history that dates more than seven thousand years, the earliest evidence of civilisation. Unfortunately, I was brought up during the war, something that the country has lived with for so many years. Fear, anger, frustration, insecurity, and doubt became my friends. It's not that I didn't have courage, self-confidence, gratification, and happiness, but these were insufficient moments in that life. My environment, my family, and the country were offering more of negative emotions, limiting beliefs, and all the consequences that war offers in terms of hunger, necessity, loss, and instability. Not to mention child abuse in all its forms.

My journey to sustainable happiness was very distant until one day, more precisely on my eighteenth birthday, I couldn't stand it anymore. My body and mind drove me to depression. I didn't know it was called depression; all I knew is that I was in a dark tunnel where I couldn't see any light at all. I hated my appearance and myself. I felt sad and oppressed. I could feel my heartbeats in my ears and each sound would make me jump. I was irritated by everything. All and nothing. I really had to do something about myself and my life. In my environment, positive thinking and emotional intelligence, even in words, didn't exist. Opportunities for healing weren't possible. My only option was to leave and start a new life, away from everything and everyone.

For two years, I just ran away from my thoughts and feelings, burying them in work. I was accompanying French tourist groups in Egypt, and it was a perfect transition for me. I just enjoyed life, partying, discovering new things, and avoiding any thoughts or feelings. I kept myself really busy. Then reality hit. The company I worked for shut down the Egyptian circuit due to the war in Iraq. I had to stop and think of what I had to do next. I had left after secondary school and had studied only one semester at university. Having worked with the hospitality industry from the tourist side, I loved the approach and the lifestyle so I decided to go to Switzerland to pursue a career in hotel management.

This is where my journey to heaven and hell started. It was the first time I felt like I was in a secure place. I loved my school, my teachers, and my directors. I felt that school was home, and I actually ended up living at the school. Mr. and Mrs. Weissenberg gave me special treatment. I owe them a lot for their help as I couldn't afford housing, and they really supported me. God bless them. On one side, I was doing very well in terms of study, my life, and my social life too. That was until all my unresolved past memories, traumas, negative feelings and thoughts, limiting beliefs, and limiting decisions decided to pop up for resolution, like a popcorn machine that turned out crazy. I felt devastated.

On the one hand, I had to show that I was doing well and keep up my school results. On the other hand, I felt I was drowning, suffocating, dying. I was exhausted. There was an internal war within me. I could feel the bombs; the horrible sounds when they hit the ground and burst. I could see the bleeding. I could feel the pain, the heat. I could hear myself asking for help but no one was there. I felt so lonely. I had "friends" at the Hotel School but I couldn't share my problems with them. I did try though. However, they thought that I was inventing stories; they couldn't believe that it was possible to go through so many bad experiences. At one point, I had to stop sharing and keep my heavy baggage to myself. I really missed my best friends, the ones I grew up with, the ones I had shared misery and happiness with. I missed my simple friends, who would sit there for hours listening to me and would do anything to help. I would have appreciated smartphone apps and internet facilities, which back then, in 1990, didn't exist, and I couldn't afford to phone anyone for help. I had to find another solution. In Geneva, I was alone, and I needed help.

The first step for healing was psychoanalysis, with someone who didn't know me, who could not judge me, who was there to help, and to understand what was going wrong with me. It was a new light in the tunnel. My first encounter with behavioural and cognitive therapy started with a shift in thinking; that I am at cause and I am responsible for change of whatever is in my control and learn to accept what I can't change as it is out of my control. It became about what I could choose and not choose, what I could be or not be, what I could say or not say . . . It took me two years of a weekly session journey to understand and scrub out childhood and teenage years, and all the recent, negative stored jam-packed baggage. Wow! How much we are and can be conditioned by our family, our environment, our society, our country, our system, the media . . . How much we soak in that can make or break us. And we are unaware of how many burdens we carry that don't belong to us, weights that we are not supposed to carry from the beginning. I can go on about this forever. One thing I learned was that when you touch the bottom, you can only climb up, and that is only if you want to. Since then, I started to look for salvation.

From my thirties, I started studying and researching different schools of thought, reading books (some references have been listed at the end of the book), attending international workshops, listening to leading inspiring gurus around the world, and pouring over websites on all kinds on self-therapy and neuroscience (Neuro-Linguistic Programming, Time Line Therapy, Hypnosis,

Faradarmani, Positive Psychology, Cognitive Behavioural Therapy (CBT), Quantum Physics, Holistic and Spiritual Development...), and I was creating and delivering training programmes around the world. I was growing, falling, and rising stronger again.

You deserve the truth; you deserve to know that you are the architect of your life and happiness. You need to hear about all this.

If I can do it, anyone can do it.

You hear people say: "This person is born optimistic or this one is born pessimistic." In nature, God created us as positive creatures. Our minds only understand positive language. Don't think of a blue elephant. What are you thinking about? A blue elephant. How can you not think about something without thinking about it first? In order to process not to think about a blue elephant, you need to think about a blue elephant, and then think about not thinking about a blue elephant, which means you are double thinking. In other words, you are thinking twice. When we are in a negative cycle, we put in double the effort to produce. This is one of the reasons why we get tired, stressed, and exhausted in the long run. The moment you become aware that you drain yourself when you are in a negative mode, in other words, by changing the way you think, feel, and narrate your story, you will then change your actions and your results, and ultimately experience happiness.

If most of your thinking is negative, then the chart of success, happiness, and healthiness, in the long run, is very difficult to attain and, needless to say, sustain. When your thoughts are limiting you with doubt, poor self-esteem, fear, anxiety, frustration, dissatisfaction . . . when your emotions are full of pain, physical and mental, what vibrations emanate from you? What behaviour will you portray and what actions will you take? Not to mention the results that you will obtain.

The biggest obstacle in Living and Spreading Sustainable Happiness is **YOU** whether you are a parent, husband, wife, child, friend, employee, manager, director, chief executive officer, or president...

YOU make the difference!

I started my career in sales. I don't know whether I should say I was born as a salesperson. When I graduated from Geneva Hotel Management School, Switzerland, I only saw myself selling dreams and making them a reality. Yes, I fit into sales, yet I had to undergo a long journey of self-development and discovery. One of my greatest values is humility. I am always questioning myself and ready to put myself at cause, looking at my part of responsibility. I knew that the answers I needed to find for sustainability weren't in the technicality of my skills and competencies, but something more profound within. I came across all types of "mentors" in my journey. Some were very inspiring, with the objective of lifting me up, and there were others who challenged my thinking to learn from them. I avoided taking them as positive role models because of their use of wrong power, their negative influence, and physical or verbal harassment.

One great learning I gleaned is that no one can make the change in you and for you.

- Where does change start?
- Whenever we fall, how can we rise stronger?

The moment you decide that the results in your career and life aren't making you happy, you need to question yourself and put all the necessary efforts to do whatever it takes to change. I promise to give you as much information, with examples and practical exercises, as I can.

I have created and delivered plenty of programmes, conferences, and talks in Europe, the Middle East, and Africa. These include: Dive-In, Leading by Example, Change Management, Happiness Tribe, Strategic Selling, Team Miracles, Positive Performing Teams, Excellence in Customer Experience, Time-Out (Stress Management, Preventing, and Handling), I wrote my first book about sales, but all I desired was to write an autobiography revealing my purpose, and how I became who I am today. Following **three near-death episodes**, I have never been so clear about my mission, given **three rebirth chances** to spread the message that life shouldn't be taken for granted and that we are so lucky to be a part of it. I survived a car bomb and bomb fragments during the civil war in Lebanon, but I was still unclear about the purpose of my survivals. Thanks to my car accident in 2018, I remembered and realised that I am miraculously alive and I will do whatever is in my control to make people value the most important thing: **LIFE**. Aren't you often walking dead when overwhelmed and oppressed with work and personal situations? When you are running to no destination, off-track, unhappy, confused, and feeling deeply empty?

STOP wasting time with excuses and start focusing on a life WORTH LIVING and worth dying for. If *Happydemic* can help even one person to get back on track and live life to the fullest, achieve their desires, and, mainly, be sustainably happy, I would have attained my goal.

"It's not who you are that holds you back from happiness,
It's who you think you're not."

Denis Waitley

"**HAPPINESS** is not HAVING the BEST of EVERYTHING you WANT.

It is **MAKING** the **BEST** of EVERYTHING you have GOT."

Oprah Winfrey

The First Step

Behavioural, Cognitive, Holistic, and Spiritual Approaches to Living and THEN Spreading Sustainable Happiness

My Personal Initiation

I started my career and adult life with complete unawareness of the importance of self-management, cognitive and behavioural positive education. I am going to take you through my personal experience in research, growth, and continuous daily work for seeking sustainable happiness. I will, for this purpose, concentrate on the significant negative stages that triggered the **ACTION NOW** BUTTON. This book focuses on how I turned negative situations, thoughts, feelings, stories, and results into positive sustainable change and happiness.

I was so lucky to have grown through so many obstacles and negative stages to be the person I am today. To just be. To be HAPPY now, today, and create happiness for tomorrow and the day after that, to spread it all around me; acknowledging, accepting, facing, handling, and overcoming each obstacle on my journey. With patience, tons of courage, determination, FAITH, and perseverance, I could break my black walls.

At school, we received the necessary knowledge for upper studies, good values, and foreign languages to be able to communicate with different people. At university, we learned to become a title, a role in the community, whether as executives, doctors, engineers, salespeople, and so forth. I hadn't had the chance, nor was there any signal of self-development and self-discovery in my world. My first contact with learning to listen and pay attention to what was going on in my mind started at the age of twenty with my psychotherapy following all the traumatic baggage accumulated from my childhood, family, and environment.

I can only thank my therapist for the enriching years of self-discovery. When I went to him, I was completely broken, confused, depressed, and very angry. I came out like new. He taught me to listen to myself, understand my thoughts, and accept my past in addition to grasping all its learnings. Yet, he was doing the questioning job, jotting down notes, and giving me some explanations and actions to be taken. The week after, we followed-up on the previous session's learnings and what I had applied and how I felt. It was quite a long process of digging and turning the soil. I went through terrible moments of great sadness and anger, not to mention how much I cried. Tissue manufacturers won a great customer.

It was a great rebirth, yet it was without understanding how I succeeded to feel better and move on. I wasn't taught the mechanism of how I could manage all that was going on inside me on a long-term basis. I felt like I had put my entire past in a drawer. I arrived at a new destination where I felt lighter. At least, I thought I did.

Life moved on with all the challenges one has to face, that is, daily life at work, motherhood, and relationships. It felt like a Luna Park being in a roller coaster, driven at full speed high up and going down fast. I kept adding new negative baggage, not to mention the stress of having to cope with high managerial positions, looking after the home, being a good wife, an excellent mother, an irreproachable friend and relative, a successful lady, the best . . . the highest . . . the most . . . Compared to who? Compared to what? Why?

I wanted to be loved, appreciated by everyone, and do everything 100 per cent. I ignored the fact that it is very challenging and difficult to satisfy everyone and do everything 100 per cent, not to mention even self-satisfaction could be tough. That word was non-existent in my repertory at that time. I just existed to serve others perfectly. Do, do, do.

I felt like a pressure cooker all those years, layers and layers and layers until the cooking is overdone; then a burst of steam comes out. Sometimes things went back to normal easily, at other times, I would feel overwhelmed and sick, but I kept on fighting with believing: "That's life," "I am strong," "I can do it," "It is ok . . ."

So many times, I felt I couldn't do it anymore; my body was aching, my brain was bursting, my thoughts were racing, they were confused, scrambled, but I would keep going, ignoring all the internal messages, ignoring my needs, ignoring myself, complete IGNORANCE. At what cost? All those years of giving up so many moments of happiness and unable to sustain myself. A draining, vicious yo-yo circle.

My new birth didn't last for long; I would say five years. I would climb Mount Everest, get back, and start all over again. I didn't have a single minute for myself. I was in robot mode, satisfying my career ambitions, moving countries, living the expat life, having different positions in different parts of the world, taking care of my home, my family, my kids, and, whenever possible, socialising, with the motto of doing all with 100 per cent satisfaction for everyone excluding myself. And I did this for so many years. I was living for everybody else, be and do everything PERFECTLY. I wouldn't settle for less. Imagine what I was creating on a daily basis.

Mood swings, depression, anxiety, doubt, fear, anger, frustration, stress, physical, mental, and emotional pains. I went on like this until the year 2000. I was working in the United Arab Emirates as Director of Sales and Marketing, and we were into sales training.

During that period, my husband was working in a different country, and I was alone with my son. My life resumed with a marathon action plan. I barely slept, trying to be there for my son on a planned timetable. I ran my department, entertained customers, and did my job at over 100 per cent potential. Inside me, everything was boiling. I was exhausted, but most of all, unhappy. I had so many questions in my mind with no answers. Until that sales course. Thanks to Ian, our trainer, who covered new ways and techniques of selling. But what he did cover that I needed most was: you need to take care of yourself or else you will pay with pain. He used Neuro-Linguistic Programming and gave me a few tips that completely shook my tree.

We spend most of our life at work and we want to make the same amount of time at home with a lesser number of available hours, which is a great challenge. This was definitely one learning I took on board.

I resigned, joined my husband, and changed my life, starting a new career in training and consultancy. Thanks to Ian and his company, I grew in turbo mode. This period of my life was a complete dive-in, but I was still missing the toolbox.

My husband was transferred to New Caledonia. Was this move a coincidence? Not at all. The universe gave me a chance to finally think about myself. I went to Australia and took a Practitioner Neuro-Linguistic Programming Certification, followed by a Master Practitioner Certification. I started my learning journey on how I can be in charge of my results by managing the way

I think, feel, and act. My life changed completely. I studied Time Line Therapy (TLT) and Hypnosis at a Master Certification Level certified by Dr. Tad James PhD (creator of TLT), and the American Board of Hypnosis.

I was so proud of myself. I started my own therapy in order to create and maintain change. Have I succeeded? Partly, yes and no. In these certification programmes, you are bombarded with so much knowledge and so many techniques that seem like a complete new language that you can't fully identify with and understand the first time. You need so much practice, and expect your tutors to give you on-the-job training feedback, which was not possible from these renowned teachers. I had to do it on my own through trial and error, choose the most effective techniques that gave me results and could work for everyone else. I had to take charge of my learning and transmit its efficiency and successes to others.

And we moved again, this time to Malta. I was in the process of change and fully motivated to create happiness and satisfaction in my life. I pursued my self-development programmes. I went on a Train the Trainer Certification and got licensed as an NLP Trainer by Dr. Tad James and the American Board of NLP. From then, I started looking for other neuroscience teachers, whether by attending worldwide training workshops, reading books, online studies, or listening to YouTube videos.

I then did a Master Results and Performance Coach Certification with Christopher Howard, UK, together with Advanced Neurological Repatterning.

I read so many holistic and business books. Some of the authors I read included: Tony Robbins, Bandler and Grinder, Dr. Deepak Chopra, Christopher Howard, Tad James, Eckhart Tolle, Shelle Rose Charvet, Steven Covey, Richard Branson, Jack Welch,

Joseph O'Connor, John Gray, Ted Garrat, Nick Owen, Norman Vincent Peale, Spencer Johnson, Ken Blanchard, Jack Canfield, Matthew McKay, Marshall Goldsmith, etc.

I was getting excellent results in all areas of my life and my success was at its summit. I opened a Consultancy and Training company in Malta, which became a leading one in the matter of a year. I was grateful to have had the opportunity of training and participating in people's transformation from chairman, directors, to employees of most of the leading companies in the country across all fields, from private to governmental sectors.

We moved from Malta to Italy then to Switzerland, and great challenges knocked on my door that I wouldn't have ever expected as they were driven by people I had fully trusted. My old habits of thinking took over, and I started another descent to hell that I avoided for years. I sold my company, and took an exciting regional corporate role in leading sales, marketing, reservations, and events for a chain of hotels. The team was a great mix. There were some very enthusiastic positive people and a few members with very negative attitudes. This part of my career was a great learning curve. I was challenged daily to resist negativity. I thought I could be in control and create positive change for the well-being of people, yet I had to accept that I could not bring about change in others if they were living in complete unawareness; there were a few who refused to grow for secondary gain.

The balance of negativity was so high that I had to take a decision to pursue my career elsewhere.

In my business life, I did come across tough leadership, a few great and inspiring leaders, and a few leaders not up to their position. There were some who cared for their people and their only concern was to develop them and create success through them, while others used their position to project their power, to intimidate, harass, and harm for no reason. I learned that by building trust, care, and determination, one can succeed.

Success is easier when your boss shares the same values and his ultimate intention is to lift you up by giving you all the necessary tools, support, and appreciation.

I climbed the stairs of success thanks to my values, **PASSION**, determination, consistency, humility, and always being a student. The best moment in my life, which signed the start of a great change in my career, was when I became a professor at the Geneva Hotel Management School I had graduated from. It was not only a school for me, but was also the school that had taught me life and had shaped my career. It was my home, my "life jacket," and together with all the experience I had accumulated through the years of my international career, I wanted my students to graduate with real life-transforming tools to succeed in their communication and sales careers to prepare them cognitively and behaviourally to confront life positively. I mean the mental and emotional attitude that we don't learn at school. My dream came true and for two years, I enjoyed seeing new generations start up with the necessary tools to not only work successfully with people, but also work with themselves in a field that requires a lot of passion, energy, dedication, and no time counting. I remember a few faces looking strangely at me when I was delivering my programmes, as they were not ready for this internal journey. I would like to thank all my colleagues and students for having triggered the writer side of me, which I had completely ignored. It was so hard for me to leave this job for a new challenge. Every part of me wanted to remain and build more generations. I was devastated, but thanks to my drive for writing, my first book was launched and dedicated to the school. This was my way of getting over this pain.

From that moment, I became an entrepreneur in order to adapt my personal life to my professional career because of our frequent moves. It was an exciting life for all the new opportunities it offered, yet it came with all the challenges of the setting up process of home, school, business, friends, and the adaptation required.

Happydemic was written in Dubai, an inspiring city for all developments and happiness. These were the key elements that drove my enthusiasm to write, and I feel blessed to finally achieve my dream goal. An autobiography that can inspire others for change. I feel relieved to be able to contribute to making others happy. All my life, I had to choose what should be said, because I was taught that your private stuff had to remain private. *What would others think about what you said? What would people think about you?* My greater intention is honesty with a higher purpose, to help you make the world a better place for you and those around you, in the same way, that I am fully dedicated to this goal every instant of my day.

I need to mention to you two very important events that shook my existence. I lost Alberto, my father-in-law, when I was pregnant with my first son. I was extremely attached to him, and his loss was so sudden. I had no clue how to manage the grief of a great support that I had loved boundlessly. I depended on his being around me. Anger and sadness filled my being for years. And I must say that having had my child helped me a lot to try to move on, but I didn't do any mental or emotional management consciously. A few years ago, I was hit by another important and unexpected loss of a great mentor in my life, Maria Rosa. If I could give an example of positive people in nature no matter what hits them, she was the BEST example. She was my haven for peace advice, my coming back on track when I was off-track, my light in the tunnel, my teacher. This event proved to me that despite all my studies, my personal development, and work, I wasn't yet in control of how important sustainability is and how to go through grief and heal. It took me years to understand, research, and apply this. Now I can say that only you can heal, help yourself, and change whatever it is that isn't working in your life, in your mind, and around you by changing the way you think, feel, and act consciously. Pay attention and focus on what you need to change in an awakened, clear, focused, and committed state.

My studies are ongoing, and I really believe there is no end to learning. I need to thank all the great teachers who enlightened my path. Thank you Eckhart Tolle for your books *The Power of Now* and *The New Earth*, and for your short videos on YouTube that helped me a lot. To have attended your live talk in Dubai is indescribable, and I felt as if I was in another world and had completely risen to another dimension.

Thank you Fereshte Kasbakhy for the awakening years, the self-freedom you allowed me to discover, and the knowledge of the power of connection to the Interuniversal Consciousness to receive enlightenment through full scanning, healing, and transcending. Thank you to my husband, my children, my family and my friends for holding my hand every time I needed it. Most of all, I thank my faith in the greatness of God and all that He is.

I am so happy to share with you simple, effective, and sustainable ways to be happy, to simply be; now, today, tomorrow, the day after tomorrow, and after that . . . Who wouldn't wish to be fulfilled most of the time? What can you do to make yourself as happy as possible, as much as possible, permanently?

"To attempt to change circumstances before you change your imaginal activity is to struggle against the very nature of things.
There can be no outer change
until there is first an imaginal change."

Neville

"**Happiness** is not out there,
It's in you."

Louise Armstrong

Definitions

Happiness
Year 2017 word

- The *Merriam-Webster Dictionary* defines happiness as: "A state of well-being and contentment. A pleasurable or satisfying experience."
- In her book, *The How of Happiness*, Sonja Lyubomirsky, a professor of psychology at the University of California, defines happiness as: "The experience of joy, contentment, or positive well-being, combined with a sense that one's life is good, meaningful, and worthwhile."
- "Happiness is a state created by the pleasant feeling of satisfaction, gratification, exhilaration, euphoria, triumph, fulfilment . . ."
- Author Ayn Rand says: "Happiness is that state of consciousness which proceeds from the achievement of one's values."
- Psychological researchers look at the two components of Subjective Well-Being (SWB), the "feelings of happiness" and the "thoughts of satisfaction with life." Subjective well-being is dependent on current situations.
- Based on twin studies, Sonja Lyubomirsky concludes that 50 per cent of our happiness level is determined by our genes, 40 per cent is related to our self-control, and 10 per cent is influenced by personal situations and life circumstances.

The search and pursuit of happiness is universal and is a human endeavour. We all have one goal in life, that is, to be happy. But what is happiness, really? Is it definable and measurable?

Happiness is intangible, a feeling that comes over you when you know life is good and you can't help but smile. It is a sense of experiential and evaluative well-being. When measured, it is a subjective thought and feeling that belongs to you, depending on how good or bad your experience is in the present.

Usually, when people are successful, they feel happy. Different people feel and pursue happiness for different reasons. Each one gives a different meaning to happiness based on their model of the world and experiences. When you are happy, you want more. No one ever complained about feeling too much happiness, yet how long the moment of happiness lasts is the key question.

Let us briefly cover happiness in philosophy, psychology, religions, nations, and different available theories that I personally studied and applied.

Happiness in Philosophy

In philosophy, **happiness** is a concept, not simply an emotion that refers to living life in a full and deeply satisfying way, which is worthwhile and flourishing.

Aristotle (384-322 BC) distinguished between four different levels of happiness:

Happiness level 1, *Laetus*: Happiness from **things.** This kind of happiness can be intense but is short-lived, as there is a limit to the pleasure you get if this is the only source of happiness. Which comes from external factors such as: a new house, new car, new watch, new job. . .

Based on the research done by San Francisco State University in 2009, being able to buy material things causes happiness, not the possession itself. It satisfies our higher need for social connectedness and increases the feeling of being alive. There is a risk of hitting a crisis when your life seems without meaning.

Happiness level 2, *Felix*: Ego gratification (**yourself**) with a continuous comparison with others; better than, more than ... It is an unstable form of happiness because very few people can win in all areas of life all the time. In case of failure, it leads to frustration and a sense of worthlessness.

Excessive focus on comparison and self-promotion risks alienating the people around you and can lead to self-absorption, jealousy, and the oppression of others.

Happiness level 3, *Beatitudo* **(others)**: This is based on doing good for others with compassion, unity, and love in order to make the world a better place. Self-focus is moved away to the well-being and happiness of others. It is a more lasting happiness as it is meaningful. There is a risk of being hurt as humankind is imperfect and relationships involve disappointment and jealousy.

- Based on the University of British Columbia study in 2012, acts of kindness make people well-liked and more accepted, leading to social acceptance and an improved self-image.
- A Harvard Business School study found that we are happier when we spend money on others, rather than on ourselves.

Happiness level 4, *Sublime Beatitudo* **(life)**: This is the most difficult one to describe. It involves a search for soul fullness and perfection. It is the right balance between all the levels but not only that, it is the ultimate happiness connection to the universe (transcendence). This desire can be fulfilled through spirituality and religion, philosophy, art, or scientific research to find answers to life questions, human existence, and the universe.

Surveys by Gallup, the National Research Centre, and the Pew Organisation state that people who are more spiritual tend to be happier than those who are not.

> "Enjoy the little things,
> look at the big picture and
> do everything with a sense of purpose."

Happiness in Psychology

In psychology, happiness is a mental or emotional state of well-being, which can be defined by positive emotions ranging from contentment to intense joy. It's about seeking pleasant moments and avoiding unpleasant experiences.

Since the 1960s, research on happiness has been conducted in a wide variety of neuroscience, scientific disciplines, social psychology, and the medical field. Psychologists have distinguished between Life Satisfaction (your thoughts and feelings about your life happiness as a whole) and Subjective Well-Being (your actual feelings of happiness at the moment). If you rate your happiness right now, it will not be an accurate indicator of your Life Satisfaction. If you are feeling discontented with your work, or be fighting with your loved one, or in financial difficulty . . . you will rate your state of happiness as low. On the other hand, if you just got promoted or bought your dream car, or you are happy and feeling on top of the world, your rating will be high.

If you were asked if you are satisfied with your life in general, your rating will be different. This distinction shows that subjective happiness is limited to the moment and is not equal to Life Satisfaction, which is a long-term happiness that makes a difference in your life and improves the well-being of others.

Why is it important for us to be happy, *happydemic?*

- It gives us a greater appreciation of life.
- We have a more meaningful life.
- It strengthens our immune system and lengthens our lifespan from 7.5 to 10 years. At the opposite end, unhappy people weaken their immune systems and are at risk of illnesses.
- It makes us givers who are happy to share our blessings with others.
- It helps us handle stress better and recover faster from diseases.
- It is beneficial to our relationships by increasing them and expanding happiness as it is contagious. People tend to like to be in the company of happy people rather than unhappy people. (University of California study in 2008)
- It encourages success. When we are happy, we are more creative and energised, and this attitude translates to all areas of our life: work performance, family harmony, community . . .
- And ultimately, it helps us reach spiritual perfection, transcendence, and fulfilment.

> **"People are just about as happy as they make up their minds to be."**
>
> Abraham Lincoln

Happiness in Religions

Buddhism

Happiness is the central teaching of Buddhism. To attain the state of everlasting peace and ultimate freedom from suffering, the practitioner follows the Noble Eightfold Path to Nirvana. Ultimate happiness is only achieved by overcoming craving in all forms and portrays love, kindness, and compassion with the desire for the happiness and welfare of all beings.

Hinduism

The ultimate goal of life in Advaita Vedanta is happiness, when one transcends the duality between *Atman* (a person's soul, immortal and eternal, the real self beyond ego) and *Brahman* (the cosmic soul, the eternal essence of the universe and the ultimate divine reality) by realising the Self in all.

Confucianism

Mencius, the Chinese Confucian thinker, advised political leaders two thousand three hundred years ago that the mind played a mediating role between the "lesser self" = the physiological self, and the "greater self" = the moral self. One needs to nourish one's vital force.

Judaism

Happiness or *simcha* in Judaism is considered an important element in the service of God. "Always be in a state of happiness," said Rabbi Nachman of Breslov, a nineteenth-century Chassidic rabbi. When a person is happy, she or he is much more capable of serving God and performing their daily activities than when depressed or upset.

Roman Catholicism

In Catholicism, the ultimate end of human existence consists of happiness to be attained not in this life but in the next one. Temporal life is transitory, and supreme joy consists in the contemplation of God, the infinitely beautiful. It's about a life of virtue, the moral good that will lead to the acquisition of an ulterior and ultimate end. Contemplate good and do good.

St. Augustine assumes in his discussions of morality on how to live a happy life and explains why the love of God and neighbour is the true path to happiness. St. Thomas Aquinas follows Aristotle and concludes with St. Augustine that: "God alone can fulfill the restlessness and cravings that mark all humans." "Our heart is ill at ease till it finds rest in Thee," was the cry of St. Augustine. "The possession of God is happiness essential."

"To know God is life everlasting," (encyclopedia of happiness). A Christian can immediately enjoy without limitation the perfect good that completely satisfies desire, and that enjoyment will not be a state of Nirvana, but an intense, free, and peaceful activity of the soul.

Praying for the hour of own death, where one may be reconciled with God and at peace with their neighbour, is strengthened by the sacraments of the Church to pass into everlasting life. Reverse planning from one's death bed will include making sure that time is given every day to what matters: the classic virtues of justice and courage, prudence, and temperance; the theological virtues of faith, hope, and love; daily prayer and regular participation in the sacraments. It is a happiness that all can find in richness and in poverty, in sickness and in health, in death and in life. To quote the words of Lord: "Happiness I give you, my Happiness I give you, not as the world gives it."

Islam

Al-Ghazali, the Muslim Sufi thinker, wrote the *Alchemy of Happiness*. He begins by writing: "He who knows himself is truly happy." Happiness consists in the transformation of the self, and by realising that one is primarily a spiritual being. The ultimate ecstasy is not found in any physical thing, but rather lies in discovering through personal experience one's identity with the Ultimate Reality, **God**.

Self-knowledge consists in realising that one has a heart that is absolutely perfect, he writes. "The aim of moral discipline is to purify the heart from the rust of passion and resentment till, like a clear mirror, it reflects the light of God." The key to this polishing is the elimination of selfish desires and the adoption of a desire to do what is right in all aspects of one's life. Happiness is not a state most people can attain; only a few people have attained this supreme happiness, which is the ecstasy of union with the divine. These people are the prophets, who appear in all times and places as messengers to remind humankind of their true purpose and their ultimate goal. They can see in their waking moments what other people only see merely in their dreams and through laborious learning. Al-Ghazali writes that every person is born with a "knowing pain in the soul," resulting from a disconnection from the Ultimate Reality. This is why people are so unhappy: they are trying to relieve this pain in the soul by recourse to physical pleasure. Physical pleasure cannot relieve a pain that is essentially spiritual. The only answer to our condition is a pleasure that comes not from the body but from self-knowledge.

Happiness in Nations

On March 20, 2017, the first International Day of Happiness was celebrated worldwide. It was proclaimed by the United Nations General Assembly to promote happiness as a universal goal and aspiration in the lives of people around the globe.

The initiative came from the Kingdom of Bhutan, whose Gross National Happiness Index is based on sustainable development through a holistic approach towards progress and gives equal importance to non-economic aspects of well-being.

The International Day of Happiness recognises the efforts of other nations who work to measure prosperity that goes beyond material wealth. The United Nations acknowledges that, in order to attain global happiness, economic development must be accompanied by social and environmental well-being. World attention needs to be focused on inclusive, equitable, and balanced economic growth by promoting sustainable development and alleviating poverty.

Ban Ki-moon, the eighth Secretary-General of the UN, affirmed that, "On this first International Day of Happiness, let us reinforce our commitment to inclusive and sustainable human development and renew our pledge to help others. When we contribute to the common good, we ourselves are enriched. Compassion promotes happiness and will help build the future we want."

I thought to share with you two examples that can be inspiring and prove that happiness can be promoted starting with the nation we live in. If only more countries could wake up to the importance of a happy nation and happy people, who in return will promote happiness around, we would definitely live in a better world and leave a better place for our children who will be "born in a happy" environment. Can you imagine what happy governments, happy people, happy companies, and happy employees can achieve?

Example 1
The four leadership lessons from Bhutan

1. *Good Governance*: The king who initiated the Gross National Happiness (GNH) handed over the power to his people in 2001 despite protests from the population, who were very happy with their royal leadership. The king emphasised that it was not wise to leave such a small vulnerable country in the hands of only one leader, chosen by birth and not by merit. The constitution led to the introduction of a parliamentary democracy, with its first elections held in 2008.

2. *Environment Conservation*: Bhutan's constitution includes unprecedented environmental measures, to preserve 62 per cent of the country under forest cover at all times. Currently, it maintains a rate of about 72 per cent. It remains carbon-neutral, ensuring that Greenhouse Gas (GHG) emissions do not exceed the carbon sequestration capacity of its forests. Bhutan is ranked among the top ten countries in the world for its diverse ecosystem, with the highest species density and biodiversity. It has five national parks, four wildlife sanctuaries, and a nature reserve covering 42.7 per cent of the country.

3. *Culture Preservation and Promotion*: Between China to its north, and India to the south, this tiny country remains on the map surrounded by high mountains and deep valleys with isolated communities that have evolved their own culture, identity, and languages. Bhutan has over two dozen languages. The government strives to maintain a "national identity" by requiring officials to wear traditional dress to the workplace and speak Dzongkha as the national language. The emphasis on tradition and the celebration of a unique culture is part of their daily life.

4. *Sustainable and Equitable Socioeconomic Development*: A Gross National Happiness (GNH) Commission was elected and its role is to ensure that all policies in the country pass a "GNH stress test" to promote a balanced approach to economic development. The GNH Commission screens all government bills before they are submitted to the Cabinet, making sure they reflect the four core GNH principles. Based on this assessment, specific recommendations for adjustment to the policies are made. This approach and concrete actions have raised the country's profile on the international stage and inspired the world on how to create a holistic, sustainable development paradigm through the pursuit of happiness. One of the great attributes of the people is the importance they place on "time," taking time to think, time with family, and time to breathe; notions we have nearly, if not, completely forgotten.

Example 2
Dubai, United Arab Emirates

I am so lucky to be able to see and live the birth of happiness and a positive lifestyle in Dubai. Thanks to His Highness Sheikh Mohammed Bin Rashid Al Maktoum, Crown Prince of Dubai and its ruler since 2006. A great leader, visionary, educator, and mentor, he believes: "If you have a positive outlook you will see challenges as opportunities, the future as brimming with success and people as capable as talented." His Happiness Programme sets government policies, programmes, and services that promote the virtues of a positive lifestyle in the community and a plan for the development of a happiness index to measure people's satisfaction.

The programme covers three areas:

1. Inclusion of happiness in the policies, programmes, and services of all government bodies and at work.
2. Promotion of positivity and happiness as a lifestyle in the community.
3. Development of benchmarks and tools to measure happiness.

The programme includes Emiratis, expatriate residents, and visitors. It seeks to encourage government and private sectors to launch, recommend, and adopt happiness initiatives. This includes publishing scientific and cultural content, books on happiness, and encouragement of reading about the importance of positivity and happiness as a way of an integrated lifestyle.

Source simplypsychology.org

This is the pyramid of human needs levels. We fulfil our basic physiological needs, then psychological needs, and, when we ascend the pyramid's steps, we aim for self-actualisation, self-fulfilment, peak experiences of profound moments of love, understanding, and happiness, where we feel more whole and yet a part of the world, "fullfilled." Isn't it what we all are doing? Moving up this pyramid and aiming to reach its top, its summit?

Happiness Measurement

Several scales have been developed to measure happiness:

- The Subjective Happiness Scale (SHS) is a four-item scale, measuring global subjective happiness. The scale requires participants to use absolute ratings to characterise themselves as happy or unhappy individuals, and also asks to what extent they identify themselves with descriptions of happy and unhappy individuals.
- The Positive and Negative Affect Schedule (PANAS) is used to detect the relation between personality traits and positive or negative effects at this moment, today, the past few days, the past week, the past few weeks, the past year, and generally (on average). PANAS is a twenty-item questionnaire, which uses a five-point Likert scale (1 = very slightly or not at all, 5 = extremely).
- The Satisfaction with Life Scale (SWLS) is a global cognitive assessment of life satisfaction developed by Ed Diener. The SWLS requires a person to use a seven-item scale to state their agreement or disagreement (1 = strongly disagree, 4 = neither agree nor disagree, 7 = strongly agree) with five statements about their life.

The World Happiness Report identifies the countries' highest levels of happiness using the subjective well-being measures (emotional reports and cognitive life evaluations).

My Definition of Happiness

In my life experience, I can define Happiness as a journey of pursuit of a purposeful purpose. I believe that happiness is a feeling you learn to grow and discover at the start from the environment where you were born, where you grew up, from parents, family, school, friends . . . When I was a kid, I was more unhappy than happy, in a country where happiness was mere moments due to insecurity and war, a broken family, traumas, overwhelming daily challenges, and bad experiences. I would say I learned more happiness with my friends and my school at that time. I went through all the levels of happiness: material happiness with its yo-yo effect; for as long as there was my need and want, there was my get and take. Life had no meaning as it was only a need-want satisfaction without purpose. I looked for happiness elsewhere. Then my attention went to my ego happiness through the best achievements in everything I did, studies at school, university, great professional success, best family, my image, but at the same time, I gave greater importance to others and put them at the centre of all that I did and what I was, with all my being, my love, denigrating myself until the day my soul cried for attention. The only way out was to be my own happiness therapist, my soul feeder, and fulfiller.

I travelled the world thinking happiness was out there, when happiness is within. I needed to awaken, to open my eyes, to become conscious with the eye of the universal consciousness, the eye of the observer and not the judger. The I that is, and not the I that only does. The innermost essence, the deep I, the real self beyond ego and not the ego I. The I that is ready to get the most out of each and every moment of every day. The I that puts all the learning as a lifestyle, looking to maximise the potential to enjoy every aspect of life every day and implementing it, not just having hundreds of strategies and plans while hoping for the best. How can you win the lottery without buying a ticket?

Develop a sustainable approach and mindset to happiness to encourage positivity and eliminate negativity. Keep the alert button on to seek out opportunities and experiences that are going to boost happiness whenever, wherever and in all its forms, be it joy, satisfaction, accomplishment, achievement, love, peace, excitement, pleasure, contentment, fulfilment, compassion, relax, silence . . . It all starts by accepting what is, not resisting what's happening, and facing with faith.

I was externally oriented towards others and had no clue or merely knew who I was, what I wanted in life, why I was born and for what purpose. Today, the true meaning of happiness to me is the ability to be in connection with my deepest self, to transcend towards spiritual perfection, and to be in a sustainable connection with God, the Ultimate Happiness. Happiness, for me, is to make the best of each PRESENT moment, give love, be love with stillness, respect unity, and have unlimited gratitude. I am in this life to find my inner treasures and inner purpose by contemplating the beauty and greatness of God, and to spread light, love, and happiness around me.

When you are happy, your happiness will shine on others, and in turn, it will come back to you. Happiness is the most important thing in life, so if you have not yet prioritised it, make it your priority now, that is, **be always happy *now*.**

Life is priceless, grow through it, be proud of your scars, imprints, challenges, joys, celebrations, and fulfilments. Live intensely. **Happiness is a choice. Start making conscious positive choices today.**

"Happiness is when what you think, what you say, and what you do are in harmony."

Mahatma Gandhi

"Say what you mean and mean what you say."

Stephanie Lahart

The definition of "Sustainable"

As per the *Merriam-Webster Dictionary*

- Able to be used without being completely used up or destroyed.
- Able to last or continue for a long time.

In my book, I also use it to mean:

- Defendable
- Maintainable
- Well-grounded
- Legitimate
- Unconditional.

The definition of "Spreading"

Spreading happiness is an "art," and the best way to multiply it is to share it. We are more used to receiving negativity and unhappiness, rather than positivity and happiness. As per the law of attraction, we attract what we project. The world is in great need of optimism and healthy minds and bodies. Share your moments of joy and the lively spirit of being lucky to live and be able to partake in these positive moments with others, making them feel better, and, ultimately, you will enhance your happiness. Celebrate your good moments with your surroundings and by giving from the heart, without any expectation in return, you will receive still more happy events to share.

What is the best evidence of happiness? Your true smile, the one that shows on your face but also emanates from the essence of your heart and mind.

The renowned Buddhist monk and peace activist, Thich Nhat Hanh, says, "Sometimes your joy is the source of your smile, but sometimes your smile can be the source of your joy."

Remove the weight off your shoulders, simplify life, smile, joke, choose to be happy, and be the flower seed that will grow happiness on its path. "Be the change you want to see in the world," said Mahatma Gandhi.

Start by spreading brightness around your inner circle of family, friends, and colleagues, and grow the circle by creating a happiness club with all happy members, who will in turn grow their circles, and so on. Our earth is in great need of souls' blossoms. A *Happydemic* worldwide community.

"Thousands of candles can be lighted from a single candle, and the life of the candle will not be shortened."

"Happiness never decreases by being shared."

Buddha

Finally, I would like you to imagine being a Happiness Magnet that spreads light, positivity, and happiness, and in turn attracts the same magnetic fields wherever it pulls. I am *Happydemic*.

"You are what you've let yourself become."

Larissa Redaelli Noujaim

The Second Step

Turning the Soil

All my life, I searched to understand how to face, surmount, learn, and grow from all the negative situations that I experienced since my birth. It took me more than thirty years to figure out how I could turn the soil and find the right seed to grow it. I am so proud to be; it feels like I have reached the highest mount on earth. From death to life, from darkness to light, from ignorance to consciousness, from guilt to forgiveness, from prison to freedom, from chaos and conflict to peace, from hell to heaven, from fear to faith, from sadness to happiness, from me to you. I can only wish that you reach your ultimate perfection, your ultimate happiness.

What encouraged me to write this book is the amount of unhappiness, struggles, and various periods of deep loss and the number of times I thought I couldn't do it anymore; yet, a deep little voice inside me kept me strong and fighting. What was there for me to learn? What's in it to grow? These are the questions I always asked myself in each and every negative situation I faced before I learned all the different techniques available out there to empower and transform.

My first defined encounter with depression came along when I was eighteen years old. The circumstances were multiple; it is important to identify the reasons that cause the disease in order to be able to work out the solutions to find ease and happiness. The moment you understand that you are the architect of your destiny and that you can change, choose, and decide your path, metamorphosis happens.

The reason I identified with my psychotherapist was his nonjudgmental ability to clarify events and change my complete perception from guilty to a victim of circumstances out of my control that I needed to accept, forgive, let go and learn from. I inherited heavy baggage from my parents' bad terms of divorce, in addition to eighteen years living in a war-torn country where danger and insecurity were my daily routine. I survived two traumatic near-death episodes, a car bomb two cars in front of me and a bomb fall close to me with fragment injury and the loss of a dear friend. I was raised in a culture that gave power and importance to men. I experienced abuse as a child in all its terrible forms, that is, sexual, physical, and verbal. I faced intense fear and anxiety, financial difficulty, and adult responsibilities too early, while I was still a child. All I could grasp from my environment was a negative vibe, with negative emotions such as fear, anxiety, anger, doubt, guilt, insecurity, frustration, and sadness, and this created limiting beliefs such as I will never be able to make it and I will never be safe, to limiting decisions such as I am not good enough.

All I wanted was to be loved, to be accepted, to be confident, to be happy, to be safe, and to have a family and a normal healthy environment with basic and physiological needs to grow in. I thank life for having taught me to start my adulthood with something as tough as depression. It was diagnosed by our family doctor, who strongly recommended that I move abroad to study, to change my environment, and that was the start of my life transformation.

My depression changed in intensity based on my life circumstances or on the way I looked at my circumstances. I swung from depression to seasonal depression, from seasonal depression to periodical depression (every five years) to a severe depression following grief until I became conscious and learned how to reverse it and be in control of my mind; until

I understood, in the first stage, how to control my thoughts, feelings, and actions positively. In the same way as I learned to ride a bicycle, sustaining many injuries in the process, and practicing until I could ride perfectly well, the same applies to how you drive your thoughts from the moment they kick in.

Today, depression is one of the most common major illnesses in the world and is one of the reasons why so many people are unhappy, unhealthy, ill, and broken.

Depression

Before I take you through the best practices that changed my life, I will just define depression and briefly reveal its symptoms and some known therapies.

How does one best define depression? If I take the word "de-pressed," I would say "pressed" as being in a difficult situation, and "de-pressed" as removing the pressure, the weights and difficulties, by turning disorder to order. I see it as the mind and body feedback that something doesn't feel right, some boundary got violated, and it needs your immediate attention. This is my personal, simple straightforward definition.

In the dictionary, depression is defined as a mental condition characterised by feelings of severe despondency and dejection with feelings of inadequacy, self-doubt, and guilt, which is often accompanied by lack of energy and disturbance of appetite and sleep.

Synonyms for depression: melancholy, misery, sadness, unhappiness, sorrow, low spirit, heavy, heartedness, discouragement, desolation, moodiness, pessimism, hopelessness . . .

As defined by the American Psychiatric Association, depression is a major disorder, a serious medical illness that negatively affects how you feel, the way you think, and how you act. Depression causes feelings of sadness and/or loss of interest in activities once enjoyed. It can lead to a variety of emotional and physical problems and can decrease your ability to function at work and at home.

The symptoms of depression can vary from mild to severe and can include:

- Feeling sad or having a mood disorder.
- Loss of interest or pleasure in activities once enjoyed.
- Changes in appetite, that is, weight loss or weight gain unrelated to dieting.
- Trouble sleeping or sleeping too much.
- Lack of energy or increased fatigue.
- Increase in purposeless physical activity or slowed movements and speech (actions observable by others).
- Feeling worthless or guilty.
- Difficulty thinking, concentrating, or making decisions.
- Thoughts of death or suicide.

Sometimes, we are faced with sadness when hit by the death of a loved one, loss of a job, or the end of a relationship. These are normal feelings developed in response to such situations, but being sad is not the same as having depression. The grieving process is natural and unique to each individual and shares some of the same features as depression. Both grief and depression may involve intense sadness and withdrawal from usual activities.

They are also different in important ways:

- In grief, painful feelings come in waves, often intermixed with positive memories of the deceased. In depression, mood, interest, and pleasure are decreased for at least two weeks.
- In grief, self-esteem is usually maintained. In depression, feelings of worthlessness and hating oneself are common.
- For some people, the death of a loved one, losing a job, or being a victim of a physical assault or a major disaster can lead to depression. When grief and depression coexist, grief is more severe and lasts longer than grief without depression. Despite some overlap between grief and depression, they are different.

Be attentive that some medical conditions such as thyroid problems, brain tumour, or vitamin deficiency can mimic symptoms of depression, so it is important to rule out general medical causes.

As per the American Psychiatric Association, depression affects an estimated one in fifteen adults in any given year. And one in six people will experience depression at some time in their life. Depression can strike at any time, but on average, it first appears during the late teens to mid-twenties. Women are more likely than men to experience depression. Some studies show that one-third of women will experience a major depressive episode in their lifetime.

Depression (sadness lasting over time) is the opposite of Happiness.

Depression Risk Factors

Depression can affect anyone, even a person who appears to live in relatively ideal circumstances.

Several factors can play a role in depression:

- Biochemistry: Differences in certain chemicals in the brain may contribute to symptoms of depression.
- Vitamins deficiency: Low levels of vitamins D, B6, B12, Folate.
- Genetics: Depression can run in families.
- Personality: People with low self-esteem, who are easily overwhelmed by stress, or who are generally pessimistic appear to be more likely to experience depression.
- Environmental factors: Continuous exposure to violence, neglect, abuse, or poverty may make some people more vulnerable to depression.

How to diagnose depression?

Apart from just the symptoms of depression, most psychiatrists believe that depression is caused by low levels of the chemical serotonin. This is why, for the treatment for depression, often Selective Serotonin Reuptake Inhibitors (SSRIs), which boost serotonin levels in the brain, are used.

A new way to diagnose depression through a blood and urine test reveals five distinct types of depression in about 95 per cent of the patients, as per researcher William J. Walsh, PhD, President of the Walsh Research Institute, who looked at about 300,000 blood and urine chemistry test results and 200,000 medical history factors from approximately 2,800 patients diagnosed with depression. He discovered that three of these forms of depression were not caused by fluctuating serotonin levels.

- Undermethylated Depression detected through a blood test was found in 38 per cent of patients in the study. Low activity at serotonin receptors due to rapid reabsorption after serotonin is released into a synapse with an inability to keep serotonin long enough. Most of these patients reported excellent response to SSRI antidepressants, although they may experience nasty side effects.

- Pyrrole Depression detected through a urine test was found in 17 per cent of the patients studied, and most found SSRI antidepressants helpful. They exhibited a combination of impaired serotonin production and extreme oxidative stress.
- Copper Overload detected through a blood test was found in 15 per cent of cases where they couldn't properly metabolise metals. Most of these people said that SSRIs did not have much of a positive or negative effect on them, but they reported benefits from normalising their copper levels through nutrient therapy. Most of these patients were women who were also estrogen intolerant.
- Low-Folate Depression detected through a blood test was found in 20 per cent of the cases studied, and they said that SSRIs worsened their symptoms, while folic acid and vitamin B12 supplements helped. Benzodiazepine medications may also help people with low-folate depression.
- Toxic Depression detected through a blood test caused by toxic-metal overload poisoning in 5 per cent of patients. By removing lead from gasoline and paint, the frequency of these cases was lowered.

How is depression treated?

Depression is among the most treatable of mental disorders. Between 80 and 90 per cent of people with depression respond well to treatment. Almost all patients gain some relief from their symptoms.

Before a diagnosis or treatment, a health professional should conduct a thorough diagnostic evaluation, including an interview and a physical examination. A blood test might be done to make sure the depression is not due to a medical condition. The evaluation is to identify specific symptoms, medical and family history, and cultural and environmental factors to arrive at a diagnosis in order to plan a course of action.

Medication

Brain chemistry may contribute to an individual's depression and may factor into their treatment. For this reason, antidepressants might be prescribed to help modify one's brain chemistry. Antidepressants may produce some improvement within the first week or two of use. Full benefits may not be seen for two to three months. If a patient feels little or no improvement after several weeks, his or her psychiatrist can alter the dose of the medication, or add or substitute with another antidepressant. In some situations, other psychotropic medications are considered. It is important to let your doctor know if a medication does not work or if you experience any side effects. Bear in mind that like any medication, each individual reacts differently to the medicine. Some can give good results and some bad results. The psychiatrist keeps on adapting and changing the medication based on the way you feel.

Psychiatrists usually recommend that patients continue to take medication for six or more months after symptoms have improved. Longer-term maintenance treatment may be suggested to decrease the risk of future episodes for certain people at high risk.

Psychotherapy approach

Or "talk therapy," known as the first wave, is sometimes alone used for treatment of mild depression; the therapist looks for the unconscious meaning behind the behaviours then formulates a diagnosis. Psychotherapy may involve only the individual, but it can include others. For example, family or couples therapy can help address issues within these close relationships. Group therapy involves people with similar illnesses. For moderate to severe depression, psychotherapy is often used along with antidepressant medications. Depending on the depression severity, treatment can take a few weeks or much longer. In many cases, significant improvement can be seen in ten to fifteen sessions.

Cognitive Behavioural Therapy (CBT)

Known as the second wave, therapy has been found to be effective in treating depression as a form of therapy that focuses on the present and on problem-solving. It helps a person to recognise distorted thinking and then change their thinking and behaviours.

Electroconvulsive Therapy (ECT)

It is most commonly used for patients with severe major depression or bipolar disorder who have not responded to other treatments. It involves a brief electrical stimulation of the brain while the patient is under anaesthesia.

Self-Therapy

Unless you have suicidal thoughts and you are a danger for yourself and for others, and if it is so, then definitely you need to contact a psychiatrist as soon as possible, else, this book can be your self-help companion at least as a good start. I will be telling you how I discovered myself, how I found peace and how I fought depression throughout different periods, through which schools of thoughts. What transformational tools I got inspired from, what enlightening meditation, spiritual, and holistic approaches I experienced, which neuroscience I studied and tested. What practices worked best for me, and what did not work.

Remember, you have the power to choose what structure fits you best as long as you pack your life with resources that make you as happy as you possibly can be, and you restrict the amount of unhappiness you are likely to experience by limiting its impact on you and your life, for you will not be able to avoid it. There will always be situations beyond your control. You need to make sure that you have enough happiness and recovery resources stacked to carry you through the bad times, and that the setbacks and the recovery time you experience are short-lived whenever it occurs. Only with practice, patience, and persistence, will you discover your deep self and be able to connect with your inner true being and achieve sustainable happiness.

How My Depression Got Treated at First

I will be telling you about how my depression got treated medically, then with alternative medicine practices. Together with some external tools I used to help my body help my mind, I decided to go as deep as needed, as far as I can possibly dig and implement my formula for sustainable happiness and healthy lifestyle.

Medication

When I was off-track, in a negative cycle, unhappy and in question-mark mode, I was diagnosed with all types of labels since age eighteen (stress post-trauma, overworked, burnout, depression, seasonal depression, periodical depression, severe depression, and bipolar disorder, and as the last psychiatrist I visited couldn't tie these to any serious mental illness, the final diagnosis was Borderline Personality Disorder). I can't express how scared I felt during each and every diagnosis. I would think, "Oh my God, I am sick." "I am irreversibly sick," was the next bad thought I believed in, and then it affirmed and reaffirmed itself. So many years of struggle, internal conflict between my mind and my body, my hopelessness at times, not to mention the profound suffering due to medication. A long trial and error path. Throughout, I kept my faith, my courage and my will to get over each occurring situation.

At moments, I would feel on top of the world, during others I would drown and not know how to catch my breath. Each medication gave me short-term help and came with plenty of side effects. I have to be honest, they had more side effects than benefits in my case. I would feel good for a few weeks, maybe months to a year and a half at the maximum, and then fall again. I would change the medication, and then wait. The sun would shine and soon after, the night would take over.

I was on and off medication. But each time I was about to start one, I had a feeling deep inside, with my little voice nagging, that all this was not good for me, that my body didn't need these toxins, and that I could fight it by listening to my mind and body feedback; look for solutions and take action. Then the doctors would convince me that I couldn't do it alone, and that I needed the medication as a little push, like a person who has broken his leg, and needs a walking stick to help him out for a short period.

Until one grateful day, I was following Faradarmani interuniversal consciousness connection and soul search. I was under a medication that was only pulling me down like never before.

Worse, I had horrible thoughts that didn't belong to me at all. I kept thinking, "What am I doing in this world? My presence isn't needed. I can't stand living with myself any longer." I knew deep down that it wasn't me thinking these thoughts, but I was tired of fighting; actually, I was intoxicated with medicine that wouldn't allow me to think clearly, and I had created the vicious inner narration habit of sickness, unhappiness, and despair. A huge feeling from my deepest being enveloped my whole body and mind with a very strong internal voice that said, "How can you even think this when you should be grateful for living this life and been given several chances to make the best of it. You are more than medicine, sickness, sadness, unhappiness, emotions, cells, bones, and flesh. You are God's creation in his image, and your life is worth living." I decided there and then to quit my medication, following a period of tapering off. I threw everything in the garbage and I felt FREE. My profound deep inner self-discovery and healing period kicked off under a greater awareness.

I will be giving you a quick reference of my medication journey. I request you to read it, and kindly do not take any medication without having had a complete checkup with a specialist doctor.

At first, I underwent homoeopathic treatment with valerian flowers, chamomile infusions at night, melatonin, Passiflora flower, and St John's Wort or Hypericum perforatum. But, be very careful with the use of St John's Wort as it reduces the effectiveness of oral contraceptive pills. It shouldn't be taken along with standard antidepressant drugs as it affects enzymes in the gastrointestinal tract and liver that are involved in drug metabolism, so it can reduce the drug's effectiveness.

Then I took a blend of Bach flowers, to help alleviate impatience, lower stress, recover from traumas, ground myself, and stay alert in the present moment.

The next was lithium in ampoules (for six months, without being informed of their interaction with many other medications) and magnesium in capsules and then in powder form (very beneficial for sleeping and muscle cramps for fitness recovery).

The effect of homoeopathic medication didn't last long. I think this was mainly because I didn't believe in natural medication at that time; my mind was conditioned to believe the best medicine was pharmaceutical prescribed by a specialist doctor, not to mention how ignorant I was still about me being in control of all this.

List of the antidepressants I took with the benefits and side effects I have experienced:

- Sertraline: A Selective Serotonin Reuptake Inhibitor (SSRI) to restore serotonin balance in the brain.
  Benefits: Improves moods, energy levels, interest in daily life, and decreases anxiety and unwanted thoughts.
  Side effects: Sweating, trouble sleeping, dry mouth, shaking, and muscle cramps.
- Fluoxetine: A Selective Serotonin Reuptake Inhibitor (SSRI)
  Side effects: Trouble sleeping, unusual mood changes, hallucinations, fast heartbeat, and restlessness.
- Pregabalin: Gabapentinoid, Gamma Aminobutyric Acid (GABA) prescribed when I was diagnosed with fibromyalgia, a weak immune system disease. Fibromyalgia comes from overactive nerves and causes neuropathic chronic pain condition that is widespread all over the upper and lower parts of the body, shoulders, and neck with deep stiffness, muscle soreness, and radiating pain. This results in sleep problems, fatigue, difficulty in thinking clearly, and in performing everyday

tasks. It provokes and accentuates anxiety, depression, and migraines/headaches.
Side effects: Sleepiness, dry mouth, and swelling feet.
- Duloxetine: A Serotonin Norepinephrine Reuptake Inhibitor (SNRI), given to replace Pregabalin and help me treat fibromyalgia and psoriatic arthritis (a form of arthritis affecting people with psoriasis; itchy skin and red patches topped with silvery scales). I developed psoriasis first and then psoriatic arthritis, a joint problem that is very painful. When inflamed, your whole body aches. Depression is one symptom of these immune system diseases. This active substance worked best for me. I felt good during the treatment; the only side effect was loss of interest and feeling in terms of the libido. After a year and a half of treatment, my moods were not stable, so we had to change again.
- Quetiapine: An atypical antipsychotic used to treat bipolar and major depression to restore the balance of neurotransmitters in the brain.
Benefits: none.
Side effects: I felt dizzy then lightheaded, and fainted after I took the first pill. I stopped it immediately.
- Desvenlafaxine: A Serotonin Norepinephrine Reuptake Inhibitor (SNRI), to restore the balance of natural substances in the brain.
Benefits: none.
Side effects: The worst medication I took. I started having very racing negative thoughts that didn't belong to me, such as suicide, along with insomnia and extreme nervousness. I had significant side effects when I withdrew from it for five months.
- Bupropion: Helps in treating and seasonal affective disorder. It improves mood and restores the balance of dopamine and norepinephrine in the brain.

Usual side effects of antidepressants.
For a short time, I was taking a cocktail of Bupropion with Duloxetine and Aripiprazole (a stabiliser). All the side effects I mentioned so far.
- Alprazolam: An anxiolytic, short-acting benzodiazepine to give me tranquillity when I felt crisis situation of high anxiety or stress.
- Amitriptyline: To help treat pain associated with migraine, fibromyalgia, and rheumatism; as a muscle relaxant.

I must say it was a learning curve to find the right treatment to heal my pain. We are unique individuals and each of us reacts differently to medication. I found the Pharmacogenetic Analysis, a genetic DNA test that was prescribed to me by a Psychiatrist, very useful. I respect it, as I agree fully that treating mental illnesses with all the different medications available in the market and finding the right medication that suits the individual and works best immediately is very challenging. The road is a trial and error experimental relationship where the patient is the person going through so much physically, emotionally, and chemically. You think you are treating yourself, ignoring the effects of such or such medication on your liver, and actually, you are toxifying your body. Pharmacogenetics studies inherited genetic responses to drugs both in terms of therapeutic effects as well as adverse effects. This study helps predict drug-drug interaction and tailor doses to the person's genetic makeup, safety, and efficiency to find the best drug that fits. I did the test for all the psychiatric drugs genetic response.

Each drug has a colour result that indicates how I genetically metabolise the drug:

- White: No genetic variants relevant to the treatment have been found. Use as directed.

- **Green:** Increased likelihood of positive response and/or lower risk of adverse drug reactions.
- **Yellow:** Need for drug dose monitoring and/or less likelihood of a positive response.
- **Red:** Increased risk of adverse drug reactions.

Antidepressants

Agomelatine		Amitriptyline		Bupropion	Standard
Citalopram		Clomipramine		Desipramine	
Desvenlafaxine	Standard	Doxepine		Duloxetine	
Escitalopram		Fluoxetine		Fluvoxamine	
Imipramine		Mianserin		Mirtazapine	
Nortriptyline		Paroxetine		Sertraline	
Trimipramine		Venlafaxine		Vortioxetine	

Antipsychotics

Aripiprazole		Clozapine		Haloperidol	
Olanzapine		Paliperidone		Perphenazine	
Pimozide		Quetiapine		Risperidone	
Thioridazine		Zuclopenthixol			

Stabilizers and anticonvulsants

Carbamazepine	Standard	Clobazam		Clonazepam	
Eslicarbazepine		Lamotrigine		Levetiracetam	
Lithium*	Standard	Lorazepam	Standard	Oxcarbazepine	
Phenobarbital		Phenytoin		Topiramate	
Valproic Acid		Vigabatrin			

Others

Atomoxetine		Methadone	Standard	Methylphenidate	
Naloxone	Standard	Naltrexone	Standard		

Standard	WHITE		RED
	YELLOW		GREEN: no result was found

Gene	Genotype	Phenotype
CYP1A2	*1F/*1F	Ultrarapid metaboliser
CYP2B6	*1/*6	Extensive (normal) metaboliser
CYP2C9	*1/*1	Extensive (normal) metaboliser
CYP2C19	*1/*17	Ultrarapid metaboliser
CYP2D6	*1/*4	Intermediate metaboliser
CYP3A4	*1/*22	Deficient metaboliser

DRUG	RECOMMENDATIONS FOR GUIDANCE PURPOSES
Agomelatine	**Analysis result:** ■ Ultrarapid metabolizer of the drug (CYP1A2) **Recommendation:** The patient carries a variant that has been associated with an increased drug metabolism (CYP1A2). Therefore, he/she may experience a lower exposure to the drug.
Amitriptyline	**Analysis result:** ■ Ultrarapid metabolizer of the drug (CYP2C19) ■ Intermediate metabolizer of the drug (CYP2D6) **Recommendation:** The patient carries a combination of genetic variants (CYP2C19, CYP2D6) which have not been studied together in relation to the metabolism of this drug. Therefore, its use is not recommended. If employment of the drug is warranted utilize therapeutic drug monitoring to guide dose adjustments.

I just showed you what the test results look like and how helpful they are. In my case, I finally had the response I always knew deep inside. None of these drugs, antidepressants, antipsychotics, and stabilisers worked for me; my genes did not want them. I took the decision to completely stop all medication after the withdrawal period discussed with my doctor.

I need to mention that together with the medication, I was studying and applying tools of positive psychology, holistic, spiritual, meditation, and alternative approaches to soul discovery and self-therapies. I had a limiting belief I needed to work on with regard to getting rid of my heavy burdens, mainly knocking out depression by trusting my deeper self and overcoming my fears of not making it alone without the help of medication.

Happiness Chemicals

"I just want to be happy."

How many books, courses, seminars, and talks are held annually with the ultimate objective being to help you become happier and more fulfilled?

There are many ways of finding your purpose: managing and regulating your emotions, living in the present moment, facing challenges with a positive attitude, meditating, being grateful, and so much more. There are plenty of extremely helpful strategies to apply, yet I always had this question raging in my mind; what if there is an issue with our brain's biochemical? Would all these mindset strategies be enough?

Our brain is the initiator and the root cause of our thoughts, feelings, moods, behaviours, and actions. Neurotransmitters present in our brain communicate constantly from our brain cells to the whole body's cells and produce results (healthy positive results or symptoms for pain). Without the proper levels of neurotransmitters, our brain is trying to operate with limited resources. Imagine building a house that requires twenty people and you only have ten. Will it be built on time and well done? Maybe not.

If we have low levels of happy neurotransmitters, it makes it more challenging for our brain to feel happy.

Brain balance contains neurotransmitter precursors and nutrient cofactors to:

- Reduce anxiety.
- Elevate mood.
- Improve focus and concentration.

- Increase *Gamma*-Aminobutyric Acid (GABA) and serotonin production.
- Increase dopamine, norepinephrine, and epinephrine.
- Modulate glutamate.

What are the symptoms of a chemical imbalance in the brain?

- Feelings of sadness, helplessness, worthlessness, or emptiness.
- Overeating or loss of appetite.
- Insomnia or sleeping too much.
- Restlessness.
- Irritability.
- A feeling of danger.
- Lack of energy.
- Distancing yourself from others.

Chemical imbalance can be treated by medication, yet there is no cure for social anxiety in medication. It is a temporary chemical change in your brain brought about by the medication and lasts only as long as the medication is synthesised to last, which is from four hours to longer periods. It is not permanent, so you should consider natural ways of bringing back balance biochemically to avoid medications' side effects.

There are four primary happy brain chemicals that activate happiness. To make it simple just remember the acronym: "DOSE":

Dopamine, Oxytocin, Serotonin, and Endorphins.

Many situations can trigger these neurotransmitters, but instead of being in the passenger seat you can intentionally cause them to flow. Knowing each one's role and how to help trigger them will make you feel good in the long term.

Dopamine

It is a neurotransmitter chemical released by neurons (nerve cells) to send signals to other nerve cells. It is the brain's reward system or pleasure chemical, a striving emotion, an anticipation rather than the feeling of happiness itself. It makes us feel good because the brain's reward system reinforces behaviours, that is, the ones that make us feel good.

On the other hand, anxiety causes an alert to the rest of the brain that a threat is present and triggers a fear or an anxiety response.

How do we boost Dopamine?

- Eat foods rich in tyrosine, which can be found in:
    - Nuts: almonds and walnuts.
    - Dairy foods: milk, cheese, and yoghurt.
    - Fruits and vegetables: bananas, avocados.
    - Eggs, beans, and unprocessed meats such as beef, chicken, and turkey.
    - Omega-3 rich fish: salmon and mackerel.
    - Dark chocolate.
- Exercise regularly.
- Learn to meditate.
- Get a massage.
- Quality sleep.
- Listen to music.
- Take dietary supplements.

Oxytocin

It plays a role in social bonding, sexual reproduction, childbirth, and the period after childbirth.

The two main actions of oxytocin in the body are contraction of the womb (uterus) during childbirth and breastfeeding.

Neurotransmitters are associated with love, empathy, trust, sexual activity, and close relationship-building. It stimulates dopamine and serotonin, while reducing anxiety. Its production is affected and reduced when one is fearful or is under antidepressant.

To get your hit of oxytocin naturally:

- Give someone you love a cuddle.
- Listen with your eyes.
- Give a gift.
- Share a meal with someone you enjoy being with.
- Meditate while focusing on others.
- Soak in a hot bathtub.
- Use social media.
- Ride a roller coaster or jump out of a plane (skydive).
- Pet a dog.
- Eat dark chocolate.
- Ensure a good level of melatonin which makes your body more sensitive and responsive to oxytocin.

Serotonin

It is a regulator for mood and anxiety. It plays multiple roles in the brain's biochemistry and is a critical component in facilitating sustained and deep sleep, maintaining a balanced mood, self-confidence, social engagement, and a healthy appetite. It helps decrease our worries and is associated with learning and memory.

It is the neurotransmitter that allows us to feel happy, calm, and be in a good mood. Low serotonin levels are often associated with anxiety, panic attacks, insomnia, fibromyalgia, eating disorders, chronic pain, migraines, alcohol abuse, negative thoughts, low self-esteem, and obsessive thoughts and behaviours.

When your serotonin levels are too low, you are more likely to become irritable and anxious and perceive the world as unfriendly. You may feel depressed, pessimistic, and have irregular appetite and sleep. The lower the levels are, the more severe the depression gets. In the chapter on medication, I mentioned the SSRI and SNRI antidepressants whose roles are to increase serotonin levels in the brain, yet they are drugs and have serious side effects.

How can we increase Serotonin naturally?

1. Reduce stress

The biggest killer of your serotonin level is STRESS. When your body is chronically stressed from work, junk food, emotional stress, toxic relationships, finances, and general life, it releases a hormone called cortisol.

Cortisol is a hormone that helps our body adapt to stress as a short-term response but is not a long-term solution. Being constantly stressed causes our bodies to produce cortisol all the time. Over time, cortisol begins to lower our serotonin levels, which make us feel unhappy, anxious, and agitated.

Help your body better adapt and cope with unavoidable stress by working out, having fun, taking time for self-care, meditating, and eating healthy.

2. Take 5-HTP or 5-hydroxytryptophan

Serotonin is made from an amino acid called tryptophan, found in rich protein sources like meat, cheese, and eggs. A logical conclusion is that we could increase our levels of tryptophan by increasing our serotonin levels.

There are two main problems with this:

1. 90 per cent of the tryptophan that enters the body doesn't turn into serotonin.
2. Tryptophan needs to get into the brain to become serotonin and needs additional help to get from your blood to your brain.

Before tryptophan becomes serotonin, it gets converted into 5-HTP, which then goes from the blood to the brain easily. Taking a 5-HTP supplement is an efficient way of increasing your levels of serotonin. It should not be taken with any other neurological drug prescribed for depression unless cleared by a medical doctor. A combination of antidepressants with 5-HTP is potentially lethal.

3. Sunshine (natural vitamin D)

Research has shown that seasonal variations produce changes in our serotonin. During winter, we are indoors and lack of sunlight for long periods of time decreases our serotonin levels. Getting more natural sunlight is a helpful way to increase your serotonin. A twenty-minute walk or break outdoor will increase your happy chemicals.

4. Massage

Massage therapy is extremely effective in helping the body cope with stress. Study shows that massage therapy can affect your brain chemistry, it decreases cortisol by 31 per cent, increases serotonin by 28 per cent and dopamine, your motivation neurotransmitter, by 31 per cent. Make regular "dates" for a massage; you will find yourself much happier, less stressed, and, in the long run, far more productive.

5. Develop a movement routine

Multiple research studies have demonstrated that in many cases, regular movement (exercise) is more effective at increasing serotonin than medication. It helps relieve depression symptoms and has amazing benefits for your brain and your happy hormones.

Aerobic activities like running, biking, swimming, and hiking elevate your heart rate, which improves your brain circulation and promotes healthy brain function (balanced brain chemistry).

The maximum benefits of exercise happen when you workout until you can't do it anymore.

Exercise has other mental health benefits too. For example, by focusing on your body's movements, it helps distract you from upsetting and unhelpful thoughts. Setting and meeting exercise-related goals boost your confidence and sense of control.

When you exercise with other people, it can provide mood-boosting social benefits. Consider walking in the park, taking a yoga class, or joining a recreational sports team with a friend or family member. Exercise classes can also be a good place to meet new people and enjoy the physical stimulation of a workout, while getting social stimulation too.

6. Nutrition

80 per cent of the serotonin in your body is present in your gut. Strategies designed to optimise gut production of serotonin could optimise your mental health. Take a good-quality probiotic, drink a minimum of two litres of water per day, and eat a brain-healthy diet.

Eat foods high in tryptophan to boost your serotonin levels, simple carbohydrates that release more insulin, such as pasta, potatoes, bread, pastries, pretzels, and popcorn. Insulin levels increase and allow more tryptophan to enter the brain, where the brain cells can convert it to serotonin. The calming effect of serotonin can be felt in thirty minutes or less by eating these foods. This may be one of the reasons why simple carbohydrates are so addictive. They can be used to make you feel happy, but can also cause high blood sugar levels that, over time, can contribute to weight gain and memory problems.

If you mix high-tryptophan foods with carbs, you might get a serotonin boost. Just manage to have a balance in the quantity intake.

Foods rich in L-Tryptophan:

- Most protein-based foods or dietary proteins such as red meat, chicken, eggs, cheese, turkey, beef, salmon, tuna, milk, yoghurt, cottage cheese, and tofu.
- Tempeh, beans, lentils, spinach, and other dark green leafy vegetables.

- High amounts of serotonin are found in pineapple, bananas, kiwi fruit, plums, and tomatoes. Moderate amounts are found in avocados, dates, grapefruit, and cantaloupe.
- Chocolate, oats.
- Seeds: sunflower, pumpkin, chia, sesame.
- Chickpeas, almonds, buckwheat, spirulina, and peanuts.

Complex carbohydrates, such as sweet potatoes, apples, blueberries, carrots, and garbanzo beans, are a healthier way to boost serotonin.

7. Dietary supplements

Dietary supplements that provide vitamins B6, B12, folate, and concentrates of saffron can help support healthy serotonin levels.

The B vitamins include B1, B2, B3, B5, B6, B7, B9, and B12. They are together or separately involved in most of the body's metabolic processes. They help calm the brain, yet it's recommended to check through a blood test if you have any deficiency or a low level.

The goal is to make sure you get proper daily amounts of all necessary B vitamins. This goal is accomplished by eating a healthy diet and taking a daily multivitamin and mineral formula.

Add Inositol named as well as myo-inositol to your smoothies; it is a carbocyclic sugar that helps provide structure to your cells by affecting insulin and the function of chemical messengers in your brain. Taking inositol before going to bed can calm and relax your body, helping you sleep better. Ask your family doctor to advise you on dosages based on your health condition.

The best sources of Inositol are FRESH fruits like cantaloupe and citrus, particularly lemons, and vegetables, beans, grains (oats and bran), and nuts.

Endorphins

They are produced by the central nervous system and are responsible for masking pain or discomfort and are associated with the "fight-or-flight" response. They push you towards distant goals.

When you exercise, your body releases endorphins that interact with the receptors in your brain to reduce your perception of pain, and trigger a positive feeling. Too many endorphins for a long time can put people on edge, triggering the fight-or-flight reflex for any small events. If the body is flooded with endorphins, it naturally assumes that something painful is coming.

How can we produce more endorphins?

1. Eat chocolate.
2. Eat your favourite foods.
3. Exercise. After twenty to thirty minutes of hard aerobic exercise, endorphins are released and will result in a mood and energy boost for two to three hours, and a mild buzz for up to twenty-four hours.
4. Laugh out loud.
5. Have sex.
6. Listen to music or play an instrument.
7. Take a group fitness class.
8. Eat hot peppers.

Together, these chemicals create desirable brain states. Experiences that release DOSE neurochemicals make us happy and want more of the same. Tip for customer loyalty building: increase your external and internal customers' happy chemicals by adapting what you read above to your product and services.

Alternative Medicine Practices

I will not debate on complementary medicine as a replacement for scientific medication. I am going to list a few alternative medicines I practised to complement my medication and when I was out of medication, highlighting all the benefits if any. There are so many options available that can help you naturally on a long-term basis with lesser side effects. A word of caution, though: try these only if you do not have a serious dangerous health issue that needs proper medication and treatments.

There is a saying: "We are our best doctor," in the sense that no one knows us better than ourselves. You need to understand how your body and mind function. What works best for you? What does your body tell you? What do you dislike? What reactions do you have? What thoughts do you have? What emotional feedback do you get?

We are each born with a unique physiology, and what fuel works for me might not work for you. Some healthy food I eat might be poison to you. I am not here to tell you what you need to do, what is the best technique to choose, what is the miraculous formula to adopt. We are very complicated human beings with a complex mind, gut, physiology, chemicals, and constitution. Unless you get to know yourself well, you will be unable to find your right equilibrium and your healthy balance. My goal in this book is to offer you choices from the many options I applied and provide you resources to face any challenge or down period in order to regain balance with true sustainable happiness.

Energy Medicines

Biofield Therapy

It is a group of therapies that affect change in people's health and well-being by interacting with their energy fields, both physical and emotional. These include common therapies like acupuncture, homoeopathy, reiki, healing touch, craniosacral, qi gong, and more. They modify your biofield using external energies or vibrations through the hands of the therapist or by the introduction of sound or colour.

Reiki

It is a Japanese technique developed in 1922 by Mikao Usui. Reiki stands for Rei "Universal life" and ki "energy"–"God's life force energy." It is administered by a Reiki practitioner by laying his hands, through which healing will take place based on the universal energy that will be transferred through his palms to you to encourage emotional or physical healing, by balancing energies in your body. When a close friend of mine did it to help me, I was very resistant mentally, and it didn't work. I was not ready for interuniversal consciousness intelligence and healing yet, and I believe that no human can use any tool pretending to heal on behalf of God, the Source of Energy.

Homoeopathy

It is based on the belief that the body can cure itself using natural substances like plants and minerals triggering the body's natural defences. It was developed in Germany in the late 1700s and is common in many European countries. For example, red onion makes your eyes water therefore it is used in homoeopathic remedies for allergies. It is not to be used for life-threatening illnesses or in emergencies, it is used for minor issues such as colds, toothaches, headaches, and a variety of other illnesses such as allergies, depression, rheumatoid arthritis, etc.

Traditional Chinese Medicine

It is built on a foundation of more than 2,500 years of Chinese medical practice, including herbal medicine, acupuncture, massage, and dietary therapy. I have personally used acupuncture on several occasions to correct energy imbalances in my body and found it very useful when I had migraines, when I was overstressed, for fibromyalgia, and when I had full body aches. At one point, I used it to improve my wrist nerve carpal tunnel as I suffered from numbness in my fingers.

Another useful Chinese therapy for bodywork treatment is cupping. It is a method that heats the air inside a glass cup to remove some of the air from the cup, which is then quickly placed on the skin and left for a little while. Then with a vacuum effect, when you remove the glass, it pulls the skin part of the way into the cup and helps stimulates the body's natural energy. This helped me a lot in blood circulation.

Ayurveda

It is a traditional Hindu holistic healing system native to the Indian subcontinent. Its origins date back to 5,000 years. It is a system of knowledge of life and longevity that regards physical and mental existence, together with personality as a unit with each element being able to influence the other.

The Ayurvedic approach is based on the balance of energies; any imbalance results in disease and requires rectification. Each human possesses a unique combination of *doshas*, meaning primary energies representing the five elements that make up the universe, known as *Vata* (air/space), *Pitta* (fire/water), and *Kapha* (water/earth).

Some people are monotype, some dual types, and others of equal proportion. *Doshas* regulate every physiological and psychological characteristic, that is, from basic cellular processes to complex biological functions. When these forces are in a state of natural balance, the body defence mechanism works at peak efficiency. But when there is an imbalance due to incompatible diet, lifestyle, lack or excess of exercise, mental stress, or emotional disturbance, then the body's immunity is affected. Bacteria and viruses will cause sickness and disease.

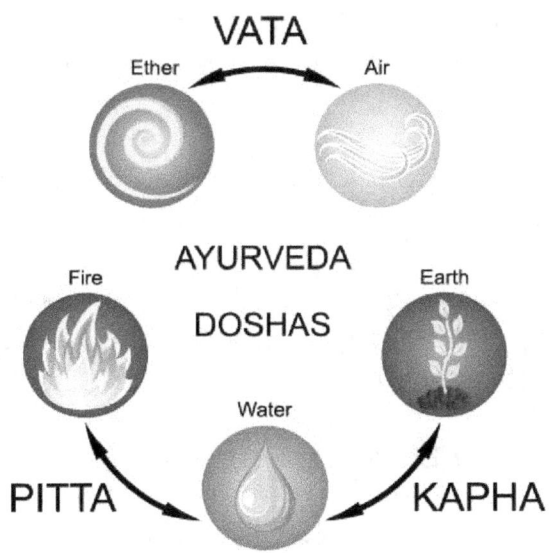

Source canstockphoto.com

Optimal health is a balance of these three.

Vata: represents **momentum.** It is responsible for all bodily activities and sensations. It controls the blood movement through the circulatory system, breathing, the delivery of nutrients to the cells, and the removal of waste products.

Location: colon, bladder, thighs, hips, legs, and kidneys.

● **Pitta:** represents **metabolism**. It governs digestion and metabolic transformation of nutrients into biologically usable forms. It also imparts the capacity to absorb ideas, intelligence, and enthusiasm for life.

Location: small intestines, liver, gallbladder lower part of the stomach, spleen, and pancreas.

● **Kapha**: provides **substance** and **support**. It gives strength and stability, both physically and psychologically. It enhances resistance to disease and promotes the healing process.

Location: lungs, the upper part of the stomach, heart, tongue, and oesophagus.

Ancient Ayurvedic sages described a checklist that every individual can perform daily to ascertain the state of their health and well-being. You are healthy if you:

- Have a daily bowel motion that is easy to pass and is without much odour.
- Pass urine that is clear and without much odour.
- Feel hungry at regular times during the day, without feeling the need to eat to satisfy emotional cravings.
- Sleep well.
- Feel light and fresh on waking.
- Have good energy during the day, without feeling fatigued and tired in the late afternoon.

- Have skin that is not dry, and hands and feet that are neither pale nor blue.
- Have good control of the senses.
- Have good control of the mind.
- Fulfil your daily responsibilities with focus.
- Don't lose your temper quickly.
- Have a positive attitude to life.

Treatments known

Sattvic Diet

This helps to balance the emotional body with food. In Ayurveda, ancient masters and sages developed a dietary system that worked with the mind to help support the individual on a spiritual path that perfected the ancient forms of yoga and meditation. It is also the foundation of many healing arts with a rich tradition taught, practised, and passed onto many cultures over the world.

Sattvic means pure essence. It is the purest diet for conscious spiritual and healthy life. It nourishes the body and maintains it in a peaceful state. It is the best diet for physical strength, a peaceful mind, good health, and longevity. It enables your mind to function at its maximum potential and in control of a fit body with a balanced flow of energy between them.

The *Sattvic* diet consists of light, soothing easily digested food and draws energy from *Prana* (earth) the universal life force that gives life to plants and animals. A *Sattvic* diet is a vegetarian diet high in nutrients, rich in organic fresh fruits and vegetables, organically grown within one meter above or below the ground, and unrefined. It avoids canned, processed food and foods prepared with hormones, chemical fertilisers, pesticides, or anything unnatural. Foods prepared with lots of love will add to their *Sattvic* quality. *Sattvic* foods include organic nuts, fresh fruit, land and sea vegetables, seeds, whole grains, milk and cheese, legumes, oily fruits, and herbal teas. In today's world with modern food processing, *Prana* is taken out, which makes it heavy, lifeless, and "dead food." With consistent and dedicated attention to diet, environment, and sensory experiences, total mind balance can be achieved. It takes discipline and effort to become *Sattvic*, but it is worthwhile as it brings peace of mind, health, strength, and immunity. However, some *Rajasic* and *Tamasic* foods are still required for motivation to achieve our goals, sleep, or relaxation.

Tamasic Diet

A *Tamasic* diet is the unhealthiest diet of all; it does not benefit the mind nor the body. *Prana* energy (earth), is withdrawn, the power of reasoning becomes clouded, and a sense of inertia sets in. The body's resistance to disease is destroyed, and the mind gets filled with dark emotions.

Tamasic foods include meat, poultry, fish, eggs, onions, garlic, and fermented food such as vinegar, alcohol, and tobacco. Foods that are overprocessed, no longer fresh, and/or difficult to digest are *Tamasic*. Foods that are prepared unconsciously or while in a negative mood are also considered *Tamasic*. Overeating is regarded as *Tamasic*.

Rajasic Diet

Rajas signifies a "can do" energy, needed to accomplish, create, and achieve. A *Rajasic* diet destroys the mind-body equilibrium, feeding the body at the expense of the mind. Foods that are very hot, bitter, sour, dry or salty, and chocolate, coffee, and tea are *Rajasic*. Too much *Rajasic* food overstimulates the body and excites strong emotions, making the mind restless and uncontrollable. Eating in a hurry is considered *Rajasic*.

Ayurveda Coping Skills

To reach a more positive outlook when facing disrupting events, the following practices can be followed:

- Regular Yoga to increase body awareness and relieve stress.
- Incorporate Yoga with meditation or meditation on its own to create inner silence and peace.
- Breathing exercises such as Pranayama to improve your mental well-being.
- Ayurvedic massage to balance the three main body constitutional energy forces: energy of movement (*vata*), energy of digestion (*pitta*), and energy of structure (*kapha*) to improve your health and create harmony in your life.
- Adopt plant-based treatments (roots, leaves, fruits, seeds, barks).
- Consume minerals.

I recently got more interested in Ayurveda and went for an Ayurvedic massage with some friends who advised me to do an aura electromagnetic field analysis test known as *Nadi Pariksha* or Pulse Diagnosis. *Nadi Pariksha* is the ancient Ayurvedic technique of diagnosis through the pulse, which is highly used in India, Tibet, and China. It can accurately diagnose mental, emotional, and physical imbalances as well as diseases. It is a noninvasive science that enables reaching the root cause of health issues and not just addressing the symptoms. *Nadi Pariksha* understands the vibratory frequency of the pulse at various levels on the radial artery. Subtle vibrations are read at seven different levels, vertically downward, that help in ascertaining various functions in the body. The pulse, when examined, reveals both the mental and physical characteristics of the person. It is then interpreted in the form of symptoms along with their prognosis, which helps in understanding the cause. It addresses any ailment in the individual with a personalised wellness regime that ranges from therapeutic massages, personalised diet, exercise programmes, rigorous detoxification, and lifestyle transforming experiences.

The test, fully customisable, takes five minutes, where the pulse is read through two boost cables (similar to the ones we use for starting the battery in a car), each placed on one pulse; your hands are kept on your knees, in a relaxed position. You cannot cross your legs or wear any accessories. Magnetic vibrations will run through your body for five minutes and after that you are given your report. It is a Heart Rate Variability (HRV) technology-based health analysis.

My test included an eleven-page overall health report including my antiaging level, my stress and adaptation level, the functional state of my body, my *vikruti* (current state) *doshas* and sub-*doshas* balance, the pulse of my organs, the biological energy level in my chakras to the rehabilitation recommendations including diet, food supplements, aromatherapy, herbs, correction of lifestyle, exercise, etc.

It showed a high imbalance in *pitta* and nearly equal *vata* and *kapha* in my profile result.

My main imbalance was at the digestion level and in the stomach. My biological aging was within the norm, and my adaptation level, my stress level, and my health level were optimum.

Here are a few pickups from the test to show you a sample of what was recommended to me:

Daily activities, routine, and diet: Follow a steady, clearly defined daily regimen with healthy food and avoid stressful situations from 10:00 a.m. to 2:00 p.m. and from 10:00 p.m. to 2:00 a.m. When under stress, reach a state of peace and tranquillity using calm music and doing *pranayama* breathing. Use free time to recover life energy. Avoid activities in the sun and minimise the heating of the body. After 6:00 p.m., reduce the level of activity. Meditate before sleeping.

Eat throughout daylight hours as the level of metabolic processes is high. Eat good quality food with oily properties. Spices such as cardamom, coriander, and cinnamon are good. Eat small portions. Avoid drinking alcohol.

Physical activity should not be too intense as it will generate excessive fire. Follow a regular continuous scheme of training during the cool hours of the day. Perform yoga *asanas* (sitting meditation pose) twice a day to overcome mental strain and to relax. Need to balance the state of mind to be in a calm and relaxed condition.

Body care: Once a week, go for a relaxing massage with suitable oils such as lavender, peppermint, tea tree, or rose.

Wake up between 6:00 and 8:00 a.m. and sleep not later than 10.30 p.m.

Meditate, read, use visualisation techniques, and practice aromatherapy before bedtime. Drink milk before bed if hungry.

I found it very interesting and useful too. Then there was a chart of ideal, suitable, and not recommended fruits, vegetables, crops, legumes, dairy, nuts, meat, and spices.

Adding to my Nutritional Therapist Diploma (Health Sciences Academy, UK), I am constantly furthering my study and skills to be able to offer this as part of a holistic 360 degree approach to better my customer's mental, emotional, and physical health.

Head and Body Massages

This is a manual application of pressure and movement to the soft tissues of the skin, muscles, tendons, and ligaments. Massage encourages the flow of blood and lymph, alleviating tension, stimulating nerves, and loosening or stretching of muscles. It facilitates blood circulation and augments immunological resistance. Combined with a nice environment, dim light, comfortable massage bed, a fragrant room, relaxing music, and oil, it can provide a great disconnection experience.

There are over 150 types of massage therapies, including ancient forms and modern techniques.

There are no side effects; nevertheless, in some sicknesses, it is not recommended, such as infectious illnesses and skin diseases.

Massage is based on four phases: relief, correction, strengthening, and maintenance.

The most traditional massages:

- **Swedish massage**, known as Western massage, was introduced in 1850. It's a dynamic therapy using lotion

or oil to help manipulate the muscles and stimulate the flow of blood to the heart. It's a gentle and relaxing experience.
- **Deep tissue massage** is similar to Swedish massage but with deeper pressure to release chronic muscle tension and access deep relaxation.
- **Thai massage** has been around for twenty-five centuries and is based on the theory of energy points in the body. It consists of manipulation, stretching, and loosening the body. It is practised on a mattress on the floor. Practitioners use their own weight to apply pressure on the energy lines, pulling fingers, toes, and ears, cracking knuckles, arching, and walking on the person's back with other movements. Oil is used on the palms and soles. It is an energising form of massage involving breathing properly too.
- **Sports massage** is done to enhance preparation and reduce recovery time for maximum performance during and after an event. It promotes flexibility, reduces fatigue, improves endurance, helps prevent injuries, and prepares the body and mind for optimal performance. This type of massage targets the muscle-tendon junctions.
- **Shiatsu massage** is a Japanese system using a combination of acupressure and traditional massage. The therapist applies pressure with the finger, thumb, palm, elbow, or knee to acupuncture points or meridians.
- **Aromatherapy massage** is a Swedish massage using massage oil or lotion that contains highly concentrated essential oils. During the massage, you inhale these essential molecules or absorb them through your skin. You can choose the oil that has the best properties to experience calm and relaxation like chamomile, lavender, and geranium oil, or uplifting ones like ylang-ylang, clary sage, rose, and neroli oil, or energising ones

with rosemary oil or decongesting ones with eucalyptus, pine, and tea tree oil. Therapeutic essential oils give relief in conditions such as anxiety, depression, insomnia, and menstrual pain.

- **Hot stone massage** therapy involves the use of smooth heated stones. The stones are made of basalt, a type of volcanic rock that retains heat, and are heated to 145 degrees. The therapist places the hot stones on specific points on your body (along the spine, on your stomach, on your chest, on your face, on your palms, on your feet and toes, on your shoulders, on your neck, and holds stones while giving the massage). It helps relieve muscle tension and pain (through the heat in the stones). It reduces stress and anxiety, promotes sleep and deep relaxation, and may boost immunity by reducing arginine vasopressin, a hormone that helps regulate blood pressure and water retention. It is not to be used in cases of burns on your skin, open wounds, blood clots, surgery in the last six weeks, fracture or severe osteoporosis, low platelet count, diabetes, or bleeding disorders.
- **Reflexology** or zone therapy is the application of pressure with a specific thumb or finger and hand techniques without the use of oil or lotion. This pressure applied to specific points and areas on the feet, hands, or ears, which correspond to different body organs and systems, alleviates stress, tension, and pain.

Reflexology theory holds that the practitioner works to release congestion or stress in the nervous system and balances the body's energy.

Example: By applying thumbs or fingers on a specific spot in the arch of the foot that corresponds to the bladder, it may affect its functioning.

Reflexology Foot Chart

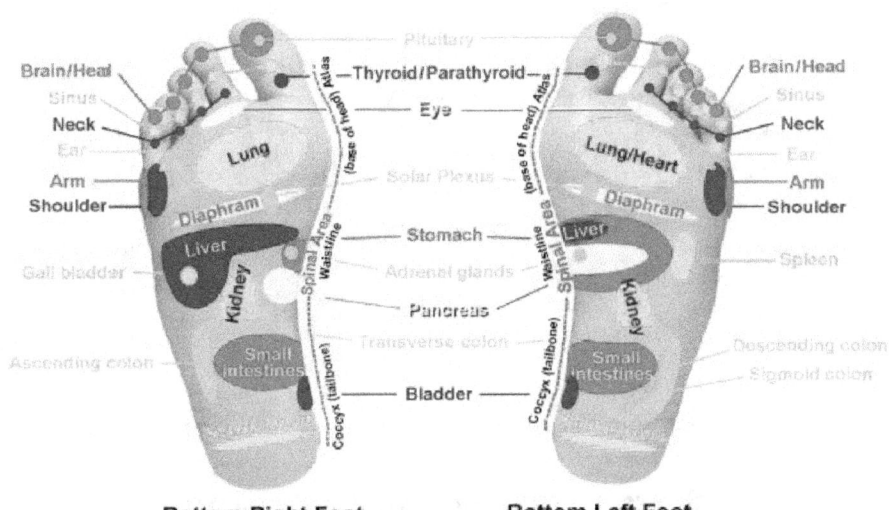

Source: Essential Oils Books, 2020

Each foot represents a vertical half of the body:

- The left foot corresponds to the left side of the body and all organs found there.
- The right foot corresponds to the right side of the body and all organs found there. For example, the liver is on the right side of the body, and therefore the corresponding reflex area is on the right foot.

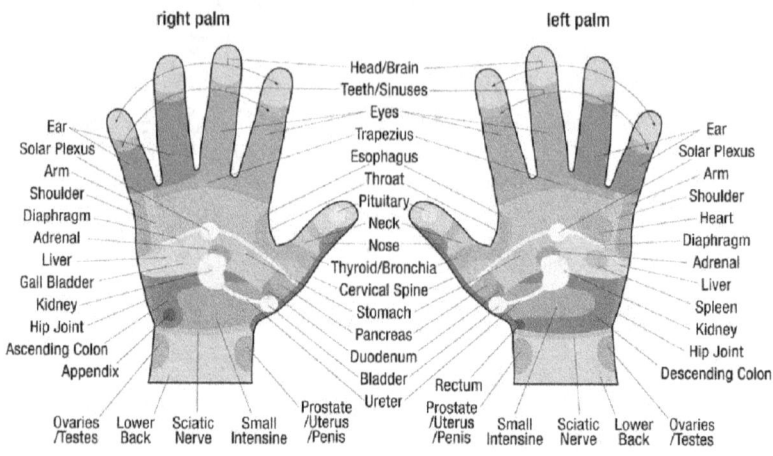

Source: naturalorganicskincare.com

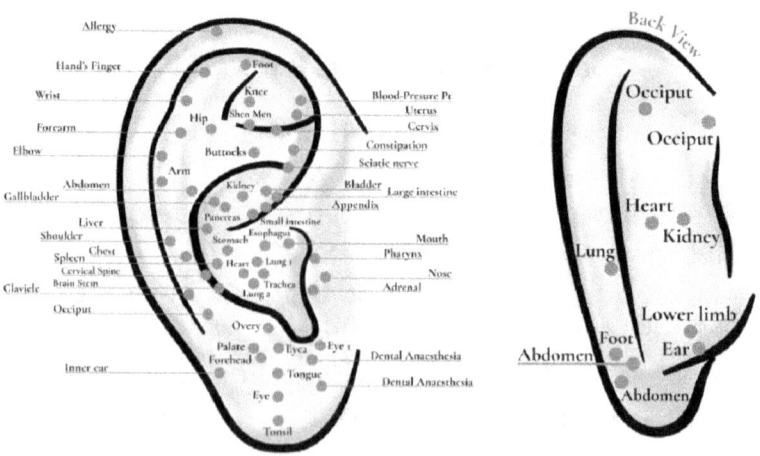

Source: gentleforindustrial.blogspot.com

- **Acupressure massage** is a Chinese millenary healing technique using fingers and toes to press meridians on the surface of the skin to stimulate the natural self-curative capacity of the human body. It removes muscle

tension and improves the blood flow, and the body's life energy. It follows the same principle of acupuncture but replaces needles with fingers. The benefits are plenty: alleviating headache, sinus problems, neck pain, back pain, arthritis, muscle pain, tension, constipation, and anxiety, as well as improving sleep and balancing the body and improving its resistance.
- **Lymphatic massage** is a lymphatic drainage, developed in Germany for the treatment of lymphedema, an accumulation of lymph fluid. It reduces swelling and fluid accumulation from the limb.
- **Himalayan mountain *abyanga* massage** is an Ayurvedic ritual that detoxifies your body by mobilising the lymph. It is a full body massage using oil to help the body cope with stress and support longevity. It's a fusion of several styles of massage that Robert and Melanie Sachs learned from Tibetan and Indian teachers. Particular oils, herbs, and aromas as per *dosha* are customised in the massage touch to your body type. Two therapists working in perfect union, perform a four-handed massage that brings the body into the deepest state of relaxation. An amazing experience! It improves sleep, anxiety, digestion, stamina, memory, cheerfulness, skin health, eczema, joint pain, and mental stress. It helps combat fatigue, increases circulation, eliminates toxins, stimulates the lymph, and promotes longevity.
- **Ayurvedic massage or *panchakarma*** uses vigorous massage in the specific energy points or chakras with large quantities of warm oils and spices to remove toxins from the system and restore balance to the body. Oils are poured into the chakras (into the ears, between the eyebrows, etc.). Benefits include vitality, stress reduction, relaxation, and a deep sense of inner peace. Chakras

need to be unblocked and energy should be flowing to be healthy.

The seven Chakras

1. The Crown Chakra
2. The Third Eye Chakra
3. The Throat Chakra
4. The Heart Chakra
5. The Solar Plexus Chakra
6. The Sacral Chakra
7. The Base/Root Chakra

Source: pinterest.com

- **Shirodhara** is an ancient Ayurvedic therapy from India used for five thousand years, meaning "to flow over the head." It is a technique of pouring oils over the forehead with the help of *Shirodhara* equipment. It is very useful for stress reduction and treating depression, anxiety, and mental fatigue. It reduces fatigue and initiates a soothing effect on brain cells through peripheral nerves of the skin on the forehead with a constant flow of liquids over the head. *Shirodhara* tranquillises and stabilises the mind and calms it. It is beneficial for headache and migraine treatments.

THE SECOND STEP 75

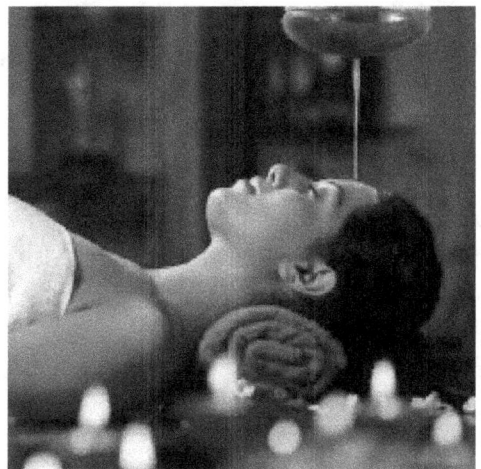

Source: okanaganayurveda.com

It can be combined with head and scalp massage or head, neck, and shoulder massage, or facial massage, or full body massage. I definitely recommend it.

Goodbye Toxins

Sauna

This takes place in a room heated between 70° and 100° Celsius. A traditional Finnish sauna uses dry heat, with humidity between 10 and 20 per cent, using a bucket of water and pouring some on the hot rocks.

Turkish-style saunas involve a greater level of humidity and use a steam room with high temperature.

Regardless of the temperature or humidity level, the effects on the body are similar. When you sit in a sauna, your heart rate increases (100–150 beats a minute), your temperature rises to 40°

Celsius, blood vessels widen, and heavy sweating occurs (loss of about half a litre of sweat) as the body attempts to keep cool.

Benefits:

- Eases pain.
- Increases circulation, reduces muscle soreness, improves joint movement, and eases arthritis pain.
- Reduces stress levels.
- Promotes relaxation and a feeling of well-being.

Steam Bath

This is a hot steam hydrotherapy treatment that has a miraculous effect on both the mental and physical state of anyone who is able to enjoy its benefits to the full. It's the perfect remedy for stress and an ideal antidote to tensions that build up over the day.

Benefits:

- The pores in the skin dilate, making deep cleansing and thorough purification possible, all of which translates into softer, more elastic skin with a great glow.
- Cell renewal, as steam has a soothing effect on skin problems, thereby reducing acne and dermatitis.
- It dilates the blood vessels for a better blood circulation by carrying more oxygen to damaged areas and inevitably bringing an immediate reduction in pain and more rapid healing in localised aches.
- Decongesting the nose and chest. The heat helps to shift lingering cold symptoms, and make it easier to get rid of excess mucous.

- Expels toxins like salt, alcohol, nicotine, cholesterol, heavy metals, and other invasive organisms as the body heats up in an artificial health-giving fever.

Moroccan Bath

The Moroccan bath is an old traditional Moroccan cleansing ritual popular across the Middle East, known as *Hammam Maghrebi*. This one hour ritual is done to clean, whiten, and soften the skin.

Benefits:

- Revitalises your mind, body, and soul.
- Regulates your fluid balance, temperature, excrete toxins, and allows absorption of moisture and nutrients.
- It also helps relax (nerves and muscles) while enhancing blood circulation.

Ritual steps:

1. Rinsing ritual: Your hair and body will be cleansed first with comforting warm water to soften your skin, and relax your mind and muscles. An authentic Moroccan black soap with olive oil is used to deep cleanse and nourish your skin.
2. Steam: Relax in a private steam room to allow the black soap to work its miracle. It will help to open your pores and remove toxins, and chemicals from your body.
3. Exfoliating: The therapist exfoliates your skin with kessa mittens and vigorously scrubs your entire body. This will remove dirt and clogging to improve skin tone and smoothness. It will stimulate collagen production. Then, to close your pores, the next step is a bath in super cold water.

4. After the bath, you relax in a quiet room in a comfortable lounge and enjoy Moroccan tea with fresh peppermint, and dates or sweets. You can enjoy this amazing experience combining it with any massage therapy.

Mindfulness and Meditation

The Mindfulness Technique is about focusing the mind on a particular object, thought, or activity to train attention and awareness. It helps you achieve a mentally clear, emotionally calm and stable state. The third wave therapy contains mindfulness-based principles.

As per Jon Kabat-Zinn (Mindfulness-Based Stress Reduction Programme, 1979): "Mindfulness is a moment to moment nonjudgmental awareness."

Meditation has been practised since antiquity in numerous religious traditions and beliefs, often as part of the path towards enlightenment and self-realisation.

Since the nineteenth century, it has spread to other cultures and is commonly practised in private and business life.

A few of its benefits are: reducing stress, anxiety, depression, and pain, and increasing peace, perception, self-concept, well-being and crafting of your future. Meditation is under research to define its possible health effects (psychological, neurological, and cardiovascular).

Definitions in the Oxford and Cambridge living dictionaries and Merriam-Webster include both the original Latin meaning of "thinking deeply about something," as well as the popular usage of "to focus one's mind for a period of time," "giving attention to only one thing," and "to engage in mental exercise," (such as concentration on one's breathing or repetition of a mantra) for the purpose of reaching a heightened level of spiritual awareness.

There are two types of meditation: focused (concentrative) or open-monitoring meditation (or mindfulness).

The Focused Attention meditation entails the voluntary focusing of attention on a chosen object, breathing, image, or words.

The Open Monitoring meditation focuses the awareness on the feelings, thoughts, or sensations that are currently present in your body, and it involves nonreactive monitoring of the experience information content.

There are multiple methods of meditation with or without relaxing music, and with or without visualisation.

In each religion, meditation is composed of prayers with or without prayer beads, such as the Christian Holy Rosary and Japamala (used by Hindus, Sikhs, and Buddhists).

Deep Breathing

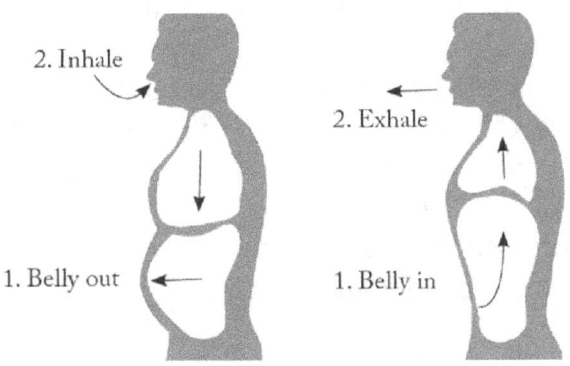

Source: neurohealthchiro.com.au

Benefits:

- For emotional management, change in the intensity of feelings.
- Self-control.
- Gain time to think about what you want to say.
- Stress management.
- Relaxation.
- Eliminates toxins from the body.
- Oxygenates the body and the brain.
- Stops the thinking process and directs your attention from racing thoughts to your breathing.

Deep Breathe Technique

Breathe in from the nose to a count of four,
Hold your breath to a count of six to oxygenate your cells and,
Breathe out/exhale from the mouth with a "HA" sound to a count of eight.

Take seven to ten deep breaths. Increase by two deep breaths each time you practice. Do this exercise seated or lying down to avoid fainting, as oxygen will be circulating very quickly up to the brain, and you might not be used to it.

To inculcate a deep breathing new habit, you need to do this exercise thrice a day for a minimum of thirty days. Ideally in the morning, any time during the day where you feel you lack energy, and before sleeping. You can combine it with a bath, listening to soft music, or lying down on your bed, or connecting with nature. You can do it anywhere.

Visualisation Breathing

Breathe in, and when you are holding your breath, imagine the sunlight filling you with light and heat, from your head to your toes. You are breathing in all the sun's power and positive energy; imagine plus(+) signs filling you, or love heart signs.

Exhale imagining letting out all the darkness, releasing the body from unwanted toxins, or the minus(-) signs.

Very useful technique to achieve a goal by meditating on it and visualising it daily, is by making the images and movies compelling with intense full senses involvement.

N.B: When in a panic attack or hyperventilated (breathing rapidly with pounding racing heartbeats), the body naturally produces a lot of air for you to go hunt and run, like our ancestors when they faced danger. Breathe in a little bit of air, and exhale much longer to get rid of the extra air without holding your breath, to slow down the breathing rate. Then you can switch to deep breathing to calm down.

For each new pattern to become automatic, it needs repetition for an average of 66 days to be inculcated unconsciously as per the *European Journal of Social Psychology*.

Self-Therapy

- Self-help.
- Self-knowledge of our essence.
- Sustainable growth (mental, emotional, spiritual).
- Deeper self-connection beyond ego.
- Self-awareness, self-observer, consciousness, enlightenment.

- Self-being.
- Self-sustainable happiness.

I will be pressing some buttons to trigger your thinking or no thinking, to make it easy to remember, memorise these symbols.

🛑 Stop button: To stop and think, or only to pause and silence your thoughts, and hush all internal chaos.

⏪ Rewind button: To go back in time and access the memory of a past experience or event, and to have a different perspective on it from a current present position.

⏩ Forward button: To design the future by taking on the learning, and seeing how it can be used, how it will look, sound, and feel like. In other words, create your future.

🟥 Go button: To take action **NOW**.

Inspired by Linda Bonnar, Author of *Press Play*.

From Comfort Zone to Growth Zone

For any change to happen, you must step out of your comfort zone, the place that makes you feel secure, stable, and lifeless. In other words, the easiness zone because you know what to expect, even when you are unhappy with the situation. The moment you move-out and will to risk, you achieve success and happiness.

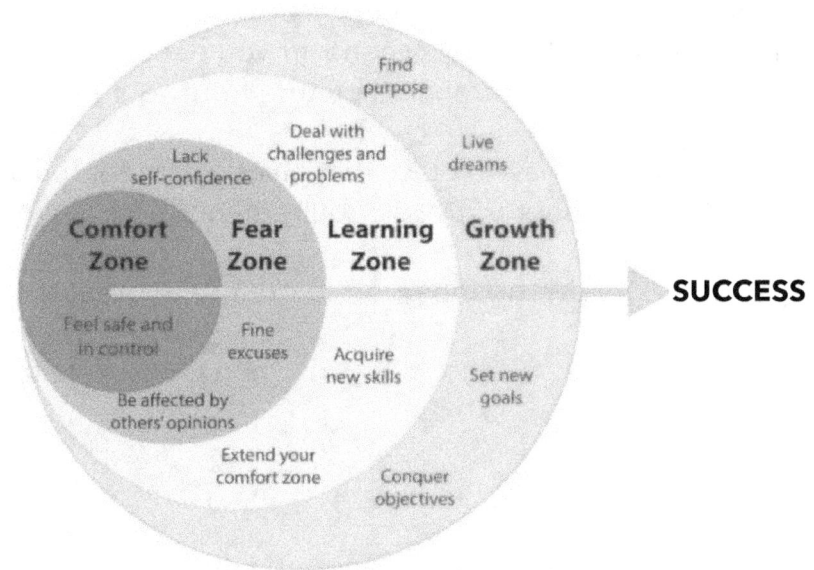

Source: themighty.com

Safe Place

It's very important, that, before you undertake a deep digging break from your conditioned mind, that you need to have a "safe place" reference.

A place where you feel safe no matter what is going on in your life, a place that will calm you down, make you feel really good, and bring you back on track. For example, your bedroom or a special spot in nature. In my case, it is St Charbel's (to whom I am devoted) little church made of stones at Saint Maron's Monastery in Annaya, in Lebanon, a piece of heaven on earth.

Do you have such a safe place? Bring back the image or movie, see it in your mind, listen to the sounds in the environment around this area, feel the feelings of safety and calmness, smell all the perfumes. Make this visualisation so compelling to increase your emotional frequency of pleasure and safety. Anchor it to your mind so that, whenever you need to feel safe, you can bring back this entrancing picture from your memory.

If you do not know, or have a place that gives you these feelings, create one that will meet all these requirements.

"Don't be afraid to give up the good to go for the great."

John D. Rockefeller

My Immune MNMS Detox Formula©

Mental, Emotional, Physical, and Environmental FULL detoxification.

I created this inside-out healthy lifestyle detox formula, proven and easy to remember (from my favourite chocolate m&m's) and by order of pain intensity, as in my opinion the root cause of all pain starts in our mind, in the quality of our thoughts, emotions, narrative self-talk and environmental impacts.

Boost and strengthen your immune system following my signature Immune MNMS Detox Formula steps:

Mind: Change your world by decluttering unhelpful thoughts, regulating emotions, banning negative narrative talk, and letting go of toxic environment (country, city, home, people, or work).

Nutrition: You are what you eat; stop poisoning your body. It's not about losing weight, restrictions, or limitations; it's about gaining life.

Movement: Exercise because you love your body, not because you hate it.

Sleep: Your best cure is quality sleep. Go to bed with satisfaction and a smile on your face; your future depends on your dreams. Wake up with determination to love yourself unconditionally.

*"Happy mind,
Happy body,
Happy life."*

Larissa Redaelli

Best Practices That Changed My Life

Mind
Mental Detox

Self-determination Theory

Developed by Edward Deci and Richard Ryan, the theory studies motivation and personality, and how social and cultural factors facilitate or compromise our will, determination, and initiative, in addition to our well-being and the quality of our performance.

We require three psychological needs to be fulfilled in order to become self-determined: autonomy, competence, and connection.

When these needs are met, our experience fosters motivation, needs satisfaction, and high-quality engagement for activities, including enhanced performance, persistence, and creativity. The degree to which any of these three psychological needs is unsupported, or opposed through prejudice and aggression, will have a detrimental impact on our wellness, cause dissatisfaction, illness, and nonoptimal functioning, as we evolve towards growing and mastering challenges.

Six theories are involved

1. *Cognitive Evaluation Theory (CET)* concerns intrinsic motivation (coming from within, personally rewarding and fulfilling our expectations) based on self-satisfaction and how social factors such as rewards, interpersonal controls, and ego involvements impact our inner motivation and interest.

2. *Organismic Integration Theory (OIT)* addresses extrinsic motivation (coming from outside, reward-driven), external identification, and integration. The more internalised the extrinsic motivation, the more autonomous we will be when behaving.

3. *Causality Orientations Theory (COT)* describes individual differences in our tendencies to orient towards environments and regulate behaviour through three types of causality orientations: (i) the autonomy orientation in which we act out of interest in what is occurring; (ii) the control orientation in which we focus on rewards, gains, and approval; and (iii) the impersonal orientation characterised by our anxiety-concerning competence.

4. *Basic Psychological Needs Theory (BPNT)* is based on psychological well-being and optimal functioning based on autonomy, competence, and relatedness.

5. *Goal Contents Theory (GCT)* looks at how basic needs satisfactions are associated with our well-being and how extrinsic goals, such as financial success, appearance, and popularity/fame (lower wellness and greater ill-being), contrast with intrinsic goals.

6. *Relationships Motivation Theory (RMT)* looks at the development and maintenance of close personal relationships. High-quality personal relationships are ones in which each partner supports the autonomy, competence, and relatedness needs of the other.

Neuroscience

During all these years of struggle, I need to specify that no one knew what was going on inside me. I am a great actress. Everything I did had to be perfect, as I would bring out all my energy and abilities even when I was overwhelmed. Only my closest friends and family accompanied me in my battles, and I can only thank them for their continuous support, belief in me, and their will to always lift me higher.

With all the best intentions, no one (except God), or nothing, could heal you, or know you better than you. It took me, and still does, a lot of daily effort, studies, great will, faith, patience, determination, perseverance, and AWARENESS, and I am so proud to say that today, I am happy, healthy, conscious, and a connected being (connected with myself and moreover interconnected with God, my Ultimate Happiness).

I took you through several external ways of finding peace, happiness, and relief for your symptoms, yet, in my opinion, the most powerful and sustainable therapy lies within you, in your mind; the root cause of the cycle and the pain reliever of your conditioned identification to your thoughts.

Let me walk you through the best practices I used to awaken and gain control, focus, and how I drove myself towards what makes me truly happy. There is nothing in this book that I preach without having experienced it myself. My inner freedom together with my knowledge, and extensive international experience allowed me to tailor-make my training programmes to help my customers face, and deal with this crazy and unhealthy world we are living in today. I will be sharing with you a few tools and techniques that you can apply for whatever disease or challenge you encounter, including the COVID-19 pandemic, and to always be prepared, empowered, and resourceful. The secret to sustainability lies in the daily creation of new positive conscious habits, and a happy healthy lifestyle.

To you, ladies, the most amazing creation of all times, creature of patience, dedication, and giving. The deep emotional seed of the universe with the greatest strength, the multi-tasker, endless role keeper, wife, partner, friend, parent, mother, nurse, teacher, counsellor, housekeeper, house manager, professional, and you are fully dedicated to all your roles to the detriment of your own being. WAKE UP, spare time for yourself, stay connected with your deep self**, you deserve it**. Pamper yourself; take time to be alone and look within, time to breathe, time to switch off, time to let go, time to say stop, time to forgive, time to be grateful, time to do nothing, time to relax, time to just BE. Discover your inner treasures and love yourself. You are the most extraordinary being, and if you feel off-track at any moment in your life, remember you are the source of giving. Be grateful; forgive yourself and your environment for whatever reason, and be proud of all you are. I would say it is even normal to arrive at a point of exhaustion with the superwoman agenda you have. When you acknowledge the greatness of knowing who you are, half of the problem is solved. It took me a while to appreciate and recognise that.

To you gentlemen, the most rational seed of the universe, with a completely different approach to challenges, and to the world of feelings. Remember to listen to your environment at first. Acknowledge the power of emotions and the miracles of connection. Take time to appreciate with your senses all that surrounds you, and the beauty that you have created. Learn to switch off, to relax, to recharge your batteries, and to connect with your deeper self. As much as you can make an amazing world around you, you can build a kingdom within. You are the source of creation, so be the source for completeness. How amazing would this world be with more of your profound emotions that spread happiness?

In order to live healthy, happy, and centred, I can only advise you to take time to unite with yourself and be able to discover and uncover the deepest potentials that lie within your true essence. Learn to take care of your mental, emotional, and physical bodies, so that they take care of you. Empathise with the beings around you, listen to their needs, avoid misuse of power and intimidation, and inspire through leading by example.

Positive Thinking

Positive thinking was a great learning curve, the NEW and "free" of charge lenses with which I started to look at my world, and manage whatever obstacle I was in control of. What a relief!

This is a way of living, a way of being, where we see possibilities, opportunities, and potentials, rather than problems. We have no one else to blame but ourselves, because the choice is ours.

Positive thinking is a tool for self-improvement and a way to survive through difficult times.

I look at it from two perspectives:

1. My attitude or reaction to a situation where things can be viewed in different ways.

> **"If you change the way you look at things, the things you look at change."**
>
> Wayne Dyer

2. The way by which I am a positive element to others.

If you think positive, you feel positive, you speak positive, you look positive, and you influence others to be positive too (the start of a positive spreading loop). This can definitely change a culture.

> **"People are just about as happy as they make up their minds to be."**
>
> Abraham Lincoln

To know how you see your world ask yourself: Is your perception of a glass half-empty or half-full? Can you fill the glass? Your answer to these questions will reflect your outlook on life, your attitude when approaching situations, and whether you are a positive thinker (optimistic) or a negative thinker (pessimistic) when managing challenging and stressful situations.

How you face and deal with unpleasant experiences, whether in a positive and productive way, or you surrender and are influenced by them. Thinking positive is when you expect that the best is going to happen, and not the worst. There is always an opportunity to grow and learn, rather than be stuck, have no solution, and play the victim's role, which ultimately badly affect your health and well-being.

> **"Fill up your glass, fill your emptiness."**
>
> Larissa Redaelli

Positive thinking often starts with self-talk, your narrative story or movie, the unspoken thoughts that run through your head. These automatic thoughts can be positive or negative.

Some of them come from logic and reason, while some may arise from misconceptions that you create because of a lack of information. As you look at your reality, which is not THE exact reality, you unconsciously generalise, distort, and delete information based on your past experiences. You do not have the complete information to make decisions. The way you perceive the challenges will affect your results.

If your thoughts are mostly negative, your outlook on life is more likely pessimistic. If your thoughts are mostly positive, you are likely to be an optimist.

It is very important to consider the impact of your perception of life as it has an impact on your health. Research shows that positive thinking may provide:

- Increased life span.
- Lower depression rates.
- Lower distress levels.
- Greater resistance to common colds, viruses, etc.
- Better psychological and physical well-being.
- Better cardiovascular health and reduced death risk from cardiovascular disease.
- Better coping skills during hard moments and times of stress.
- Mental clarity and focus.

Neuro-Linguistic Programming

*"We don't experience the world as it is,
We experience the world as we are."*

Inspired by Anaïs Nin

"Happiness" is a challenging word to define, understand, achieve, and sustain, let alone measure. I have been in the consultancy and coaching business for the past fourteen years. Throughout my career, when I asked my clients and students what was the most important thing to them, the answer was, most often, to be happier, healthier, to manage stress, and to have strong bonds at work, and with friends and family. My journey to self-therapy started with neuro-linguistic programming back in 2000 in Al Ain, in the United Arab Emirates. I could only go in-depth when we were transferred to New Caledonia, an hour away from Sydney and Brisbane, where I could finally go through the NLP Practitioner Certification followed by Master Certification, and then Licensed NLP Trainer from the American Board of NLP, and Dr. Tad James.

I was pregnant with my second child when I took my Practitioner Programme. Between my hormones and my internal state, I thought I would burst and that my child would come out directly from my stomach. I was very worried about what I was injecting in him in terms of my disturbed state of mind. The first thing I needed to understand was whether I was in the right place for change. It was indeed a great first step to understand how everything is connected between my mind, inner language, and emotions, and how that connection affected my thoughts, my body, my behaviour, my results, and my performance, Actually, it was a vicious circle; if the start was positive, the end result was positive too. If, on the contrary, it was negative, then obviously the whole circle would be negative.

We will look at the world from a different perspective, stepping out from our comfort zone, and reaching deep down inside ourselves to pull out the necessary resources to break through any limitation, fear and commit to learning and growth.

There are so many insights I took from my NLP certifications. I applied several of the techniques as self-therapy. Based on the results I achieved, I applied these tools in my corporate programmes to help others create change. In my coaching career, I always taught what I tried and could measure its results. I needed to be able to see, hear, feel, taste, and sense all the processes in order to deliver the message to others with **passion and care**. Let's look at a few psychological approaches to communication, power of focus, and self-improvement that worked well for me at first as self-therapy, then in my career as a Happiness, and Confidence-Building Master and Executive Leadership Coach. I trust that it will work well for you too. NLP can help you interrupt old and limiting patterns in order to tap into the power of consciousness and your unlimited inner potential. If you chose consciously to use its power, your life can transform, and achieving a happier life becomes accessible, without the use of any medication.

The only side effect I see in this complementary psychotherapy and personal development science, is you not committing 100 per cent to practice what you learn, holding on for secondary gains, or giving up the new learning pattern before it becomes a habit.

As we are mentally different, the way we experience life and give it meaning also differ. Choose the practises that fit you best.

One of the most powerful life skills you can possess is the ability to control your response to people and events around you. NLP explores HOW you think and feel, and not WHAT you think and feel in terms of content. It examines the "inner" language you use to interpret your experiences, YOUR REALITY of the world.

It allows you more conscious choice over what you think, feel, do, and the ways you act, increasing your ability to achieve your goals and enhance your performance by reaching your optimal potential. And because NLP techniques are easy to understand and use, you can begin immediately to:

"See life with new eyes, and experience life elseways."

Larissa Redaelli

Every situation involves people (close family, friends, colleagues, managers, etc.) and a sequence of events (pleasant or unpleasant), thoughts (helpful or unhelpful), feelings (empowering or limiting), actions (success or failure), reactions (good or bad) and performance (optimal or low). You begin to see the different elements in each situation that make up the system. You will be able to identify which of the elements are working for you, and which ones are not, to take action, change what is not working for you, and be in control now of your future.

NLP techniques are based on the concept that you already have all the internal resources and capabilities you need to create change in your life, and the lives of those around you. It gives you the ability to choose and access automatically an emotional or mental state, and hold it for as long as you want, whenever you want, maintaining a focused state of awareness, concentration, confidence, enthusiasm, inspiration, motivation, influence, learning, and happiness.

NLP's five principles for success

1- Know what you want to achieve precisely. Set your goal, your purpose, then plan.

"Purpose fuels passion."

Anan El-Bossiely

2- Take action to achieve your goal. Get started.

3- Evaluate the changes produced by your actions. Be alert and keep all your senses open, "use the power of observation, sensory acuity, and listening," to notice what you get.

4- Have behavioural flexibility and keep changing your action plan until you get what you want.

5- Operate from a physiology and psychology of Excellence.

The way I made it work best for me:

- Making sure I am supporting a healthy mental state: eating well, exercising, drinking plenty of water, getting sun exposure, being outside when I don't feel good.
- Learning from my setbacks, and through courage, patience, persistence, discipline, and practice, I change.
- Motivating myself and others, even when I didn't feel like it.
- Surrounding myself with people who lift me higher. Letting go of the toxic negative people who drain (ed) me and put me down, even unintentionally.
- Having peace of mind, even under stress.
- Being self-confident in any situation.
- Remembering that reality is objective, and my experience is subjective, therefore it is definitely not THE absolute reality.

- Deconstructing problems, and reconstructing solutions with a sense of humility, a great willingness to change, and FULLY committing to expand my experience of life.
- Aligning my conscious intention with my unconscious resources for congruency.
- Driven by my values and passion.
- Never giving up.

Ken Keyes wrote: "Your predictions and expectations are self-fulfilling. Since your consciousness (thoughts) creates your universe, all you have to do to change your world is to change your consciousness!"

NLP Definition

Neuro

- The study of the nervous system, how it takes in "reality" made out from the information we receive and our experience through our five senses: sight ("Visual"), sound ("Auditory"), smell ("Olfactory"), taste ("Gustatory"), touch and feeling ("Kinesthetic").
- Understanding how the body and mind neurology work. How we create neuro-associations of thoughts and emotions, to better direct them, mainly when negative adversity, disruption, loss and limiting events occur in our life. Moving towards effective thinking and feeling, in order to achieve desired results, and a happy life.
- How to create new neurological pathways that free us from our mental boundary conditions, wrong identifications, misinterpretations, limitations, and blockages.

Linguistic

- Become aware of how communication occurs within the self and with others.
- Conscious awareness of the language we use to guide our mind towards our objectives and towards change, rather than being consumed by unconscious thinking.
- How do we interpret events and information we receive, that in turn lead to behaviour and results? Then how do we communicate those thoughts to others?
- What thoughts will become our experience of life (positive or negative, empowering or limiting), our reality?
- What scenarios, movies, pictures, sounds, tastes, smells, feelings, and sensations inhabit our mind? Are they fiction of our mind or a reflection of reality?
- How do we narrate our story? What is happening in our life? How do we justify ourselves? What words do we use? (Do they build and empower, or limit, block, and destroy us?)

Our thoughts are composed of:

- Pictures, sounds, tastes, smells and feelings.
- Internal dialogue or self-talk (words and voice quality).

Programming

Understand that our mind functions like a computer, with thought patterns as the "software." Discovering what programmes are determining our current experience of reality and our results, and how we can use specific tools to deprogramme, and delete conditioned programmes that are limiting us (installed by society, systems, environments, family, us, our past experiences/memories unconsciously).

Reprogramme, upgrade, and install new "software" with learning programmes for conscious realisation, and coping strategies for optimal performance, well-being, and happiness.

Becoming aware of how we filter the outside world through our values, beliefs, memories, decisions, attitudes, time, space, and matter.

Like an owner's manual for the mind for accelerated results, NLP gives you effective ways to produce changes in your life.

For NLP to be most effective, the techniques need to be applied regularly or as needed. It's about expanding your awareness and developing your self-knowledge, and personality to nourish attitude and well-being. You will be able to gain the confidence to easily express yourself and your opinions, make good choices, create instant rapport with others, and live through conscious creation on the road to happiness and success.

There are many similar neuroscience available; they use different wordings and techniques, yet all relate to the common goal of being consciously in charge of your mind, emotions, actions, choices, and decisions.

NLP Brief History

NLP is a hybrid science developed in the early 1970s by computer scientist Richard Bandler and linguist John Grinder, and was recognised as of 1975. They studied three therapists with excellent results that transformed their clients' ways of thinking, feeling, and behaving. They modelled family therapist Virginia Satir, Gestalt therapist Fritz Perls, and hypnotherapist Milton Erickson who legitimised hypnotherapy as a healing treatment modality accepted by the American Medical Association. They were producing miraculous results with their clients, so Bandler and Grinder looked at what transpired in the minds and bodies of patients at the moment a change occurred. They asked what specifically caused the change. They also examined what was occurring in the minds and bodies of the therapists, and how they could replicate a therapeutic process to teach others step-by-step how to achieve the exact results quicker. The techniques developed are so concise and effective that the behavioural change that used to take years can now occur within a matter of hours or minutes. Since its inception, NLP has proved to be a reliable and fast way for people to gain control of their minds, and therefore their results, when used ethically.

Some NLP Benefits in Business

You can set up new behaviour patterns and gain control over your life, achieve furthermore in your career, improve your relationships, and add happiness to your life.

We face significant challenges and struggles at some points in our life, be it in our career, finances, health, relationships, natural disasters, or pandemics, which bring chaos, loss, and uncertainty. We also have periods in our life when we feel happy, healthy, and confident. Often, we feel we are doing well on the outside, we have a good job, a nice family and we are healthy, but on the inside, we are confused, in conflict, stressed, anxious, and overwhelmed.

Neuro-linguistic programming helps you become aware of the areas where things are not working the way you want, where you feel stuck, unhappy, and limited. You can eradicate negative thinking and unhelpful behaviours, uncover unconscious decisions you took in the past, and clear them in order to move forward, actualise your goals, and live a sustainable happier life.

Change unfolds from the inside out.

Sales people

- Quickly build long-term relationships with customers, focused on trust and the feeling that they have met before.
- Discover words that can match people's immediate understanding.
- Conscious to unconscious mind; open communication and rapport built at a deeper level, with no resistance.
- Turn objections into solutions.
- Leave customers feeling good and wanting more.
- Increase performance and transaction results.
- Take control and find work-life balance.
- Model top leaders' thinking and emotional patterns, and more . . .

Trainers and Educators

- Instantly grab attention.
- Gain the respect and affection of students.
- Quickly identify and overcome learning disabilities.
- Use new impactful learning channels.
- Inspire learning and growth.
- Teach more effectively using storytelling, analogies, and metaphors.
- Communicate clearly with ease.
- Share with empathy, and more . . .

Managers and Entrepreneurs

- Overcome operational challenges with creativity.
- Empower staff to make more productive and profitable decisions.
- Create stronger team cohesion and build motivation.
- Evaluate situations and decide on solutions in less time, and with greater confidence.
- Lead by example through self-leadership, first for positive change, then a spread in the company's culture and teams (inspirational leadership based on care and empathy).
- Create an accountability mindset for results.
- Clear vision, focus, and goals.
- Emotional and thinking management for success, and more...

Counsellors, Consultants, Life Coaches, and Mental Health Professionals

- Use the most effective catalyst processes from the best therapists in the field.
- Swiftly shift client perspectives to enable "instant" relief.
- Uncover hidden dysfunctional strategies within minutes using eye-accessing cues.
- Create outcome-oriented processes that deliver real-world results, and more...

Performers and Athletes

- Model champions efficiently.
- Develop a "winner's mindset and attitude."
- Gain focus and self-confidence in every competitive situation.

- Banish self-doubt completely.
- Visualise the path to success with greater clarity, and more . . .

Parents and Teachers

- Instill positive education and self-confidence from a young age, to learn how to face challenges.
- Inspire and lead children by example.
- Enhance children's learning capacities.
- Strengthen and empower children to choose their path.
- Teach children to focus on the real-world results, with a positive and opportunity-oriented self-leadership outlook.

Additional NLP Benefits

1. Supports weight loss
The eating habits of problem eaters can have more to do with what's going on in their heads, than their appetite. Psychological behavioural modification can be helpful for reducing how much a person eats, and increasing how often they exercise.

2. Promotes learning
Learning can be tough, and feeling discouraged can make it tougher. NLP may be helpful for improving self-esteem in children with dyslexia, by helping to provide a deeper sense of relaxation and lower anxiety level, possibly impacting learning capabilities.

3. Helps reduce anxiety
Combining relaxation and guided imagery calm anxious feelings.

4. Supports a balanced mood
Depression involves a multitude of personal factors that are unique to the person, and the approach for dealing with it needs to be multifaceted, and specifically tailored to the individual. NLP may offer positive benefits to an overall solution.

5. Helps you get over bad habits
One of the best ways to get rid of a bad habit is to replace it with a new helpful habit. NLP is one of the best methods for helping people do that. Since NLP has no side effects, it is a great tool to have in your arsenal for fighting bad habits, like complaining, judging, eating junk food, biting your nails, or putting off exercising.

6. Improves memory and focus.

Why settle for less?

We function better and feel much happier when we are part of a community. When using NLP for happiness, rapport is one of the most important factors in establishing fulfilling relationships with the people around you. Feelings of belonging and being valued help you feel relaxed, safe, and able to communicate your true feelings and desires. Conversation, interactions (both verbal and nonverbal) form the bonds with others, building healthy and strong companionship. A diversity of people in your circle can help you expand your own views, and see life from a whole new perspective. Happy people have learned the value of camaraderie and friendship. Happy people know that the bonds they form with others help mould them into the person they want to be.

> **"If you want to go fast, go alone.
> If you want to go far, go together."**
>
> African Proverb

You may believe you have developed thinking and behaviour patterns that cannot be broken. Your father did it. Your grandfather did it. Now you have become the legacy bearer. Maybe your parents told you, "Don't make the same mistakes I made." NLP allows you to connect with yourself and uncover your deeper needs. You realise that you don't have to believe every thought that rises in your mind, and that you must bring awareness to your thought process. It is a good tool to turn the soil in your inner garden, and plant new healthy seeds, nourish old seeds with learning, and grow.

Mindset and Behaviour

In order to understand how we can run our brain and direct our thoughts, feelings, and actions to take control of our life, we need to comprehend how our brain functions, and its role. We cannot direct others' behaviour with the speed, certainty, and efficiency with which we control our own results.

Brain Hemispheres

CONSCIOUS MIND
Left side

UNCONSCIOUS MIND
Right side

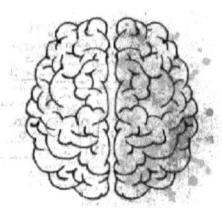

Source: bridgingthegaps.com

Upper Hemisphere

. Logic
. Analytic
. Numbers
. Calculation
. Thinking
. Direction
. Control

. Creativity
. New ideas
. Innovation
. Memories
. Learning
. Habit
. Past experiences

Lower Hemisphere

. Organisation
. Details
. Processes

. Intuition
. Instinct
. Emotion
. People
. Caring

Aware Mind
. Attention and focus

. Limited
10 per cent of brain capacity used

Unaware Mind
. Automatism
. Energy
. Unlimited
90 per cent resources to tap into

The Ship Analogy

In order to understand the relationship between the conscious and unconscious mind, I will use the analogy of a ship at sea. Who drives the ship? The captain or the crew?

The captain is in charge, and the crew follows his directions. If the captain wants to turn the ship, I doubt he will steer or helm it. When the captain wants to change direction, he just gives the orders and instructions, and the crew will do the work, and look for the resources. Think of the relationship between the conscious and the unconscious mind as being the captain and the crew at sea. If the crew loses respect or falls out with the captain, what would be the extreme result? Mutiny. Don't we get this in our own lives? When the captain says (10 per cent of you), "I want to be happy," what happens at the crew level (90 per cent of you)?

- Is there anger at your parents because they didn't make you happy?
- Or jealousy towards people who are happy?
- Or fear of being happy?
- Or a heavy past with negative memories?
- Or stress?
- Or guilt at being happy when someone in your close family is unhappy?
- Or false associations such as "I am not worthy?"
- Or limiting decisions such as thinking that happiness and money don't go hand in hand?

How congruently do you move towards that goal? Well, 10 per cent of you is moving towards happiness, and 90 per cent is going everywhere but. In NLP, this is called an incongruent forward motion, and, to a large extent, that is one of the major reasons why people have the challenges they have in their lives. This works cross contextually, if you say you want to have a great relationship, but at the unconscious level you have self-esteem issues, or anger that you project on to the relationship, this is going to affect your ability to maintain this relationship.

NLP is about aligning your conscious intention with your unconscious resources for congruency, and bringing back rapport between the two minds. All true changes happen at the unconscious level. We have had the other experience as well, where we have changed things in our life, and when we did that, the change happened instantaneously. That is how quick change occurs at the unconscious level when it does. We can all think of behaviours we used to do in the past and we would never do anymore. Why? Because we have changed at the unconscious level, and that is a congruent change. We can change our focus.

Conscious mind	**Unconscious mind**
Captain	**Crew**

Be the captain in charge of your ship and in control of your results.

Role of the unconscious mind:

- Stores memories: temporal and atemporal. Organises your memories according to a subject, memories of a pleasant event, anger, happiness, education, family . . .
- The domain of emotions represses memories with unresolved negative emotions, and presents repressed memories to your conscious mind for resolution.
- Runs your body and preserves it from sicknesses.

- Likes to follow orders, to be directed. Like with a seven-year-old child; to get something from him, you need to be very specific. It works on the principle of least effort.
- Transmits perceptions (thoughts) to the conscious mind through pictures, sounds, feelings, or self-talk.
- Learns and communicates symbolically to the conscious mind through dreams and intuition.
- Generates, stores, distributes, and transmits energy.
- Maintains instincts and generates habits. Needs repetition until a habit is installed.
- Programmed to continually seek for more.
- Does not process negatively by nature. In order to understand negative messages, it needs to double process, using twice the effort. Example: Don't use this door. The first thing you are tempted to do is to use this door, then you think, "I was told not to use this door." Our unconscious mind only processes positive direct messages like **what to do,** rather than what not to do.

The first learning I got here was the unlimitedness of my potential. Before I look for an answer on the outside, I needed to change this habit by first going inside, and access my inner storage box (unconscious mind resources) in order to direct my focus on what needs to be thought, felt, and done.

We go through four stages before we learn something and this learning becomes a habit. Consider positive and negative habits.

Before we learned to drive a car, we had to learn to crawl, to stand up, to walk, to run, to ride a bike . . . At the first stage, our unconscious mind is incompetent; we don't know that we don't know. Then we decide we need to learn to drive; we consciously decide, but we are still incompetent; we know that we don't know. In the next stage, we consciously practice to become competent, with success and failures, trials and errors. The more we practice, the habit gets installed. And this the fourth stage, where our learning becomes unconsciously competent, which means that we do things automatically, as second nature. We just forget that we know. We drive answering our phone, or message someone, we put music on and at the same time we apply makeup. What is the danger of remaining at stage four?

- We become careless.
- We take shortcuts.
- We take things for granted.
- We do things too fast.
- We break rules.
- We lack concentration.
- We lack focus.
- We take uncalculated risks.

What is the ultimate danger? **WE CRASH**.

This is why we need to consciously work and build rapport with our unconscious mind to redirect it when needed, direct it at other times, or come back on track and focus. We need to be between stage three and stage four.

As much as we create habits, we can uncreate habits by installing new patterns. I am mainly talking about negative habits and behaviours that ultimately will drive us to a crash. Sometimes unlearning is necessary.

We have six wealth areas in life:

1. Career
2. Relationships
3. Health nutrition, and fitness

4. Personal development
5. Spiritual
6. Financial.

Before you continue reading, I would recommend you stop for a few minutes to reflect. Pick one area of your life where you are not living up to your full potential, what you perceive to be "missing," and where you feel unhappy, in order to break through using the upcoming techniques. Remember that we are holistic beings; the area of change chosen will affect the other areas for positive change.

Turn the soil and transform NOW.

The Wheel of Life

Identify which area of your life would benefit from you working on it NOW.

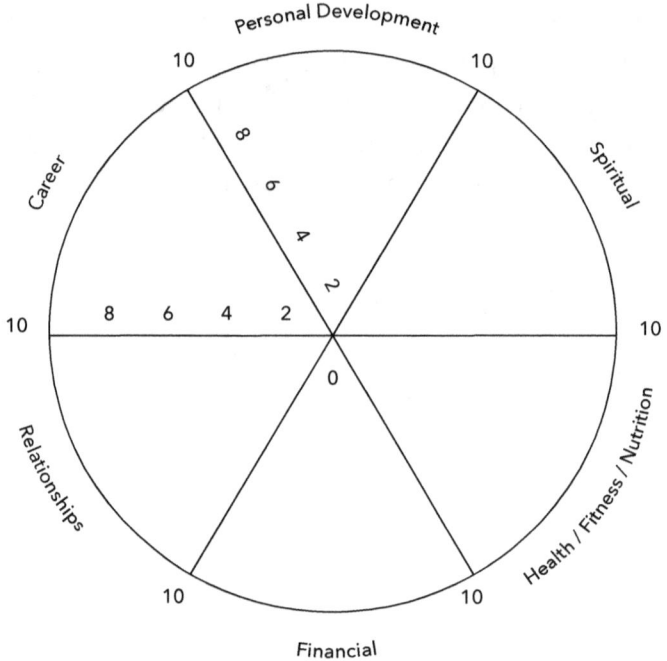

Rating
0 completely unsatisfied
10 extremely satisfied

Give an average rating to each area in terms of your satisfaction. How satisfied are you at the moment in your life? Which parts are not the way you wish them to be? Colour each area rated from 0 to your given number. For example, if you rated career 6, colour the cone from 0 to 6 in the career portion of the wheel. Then compare the whole wheel. Which area is the smallest portion you would like to concentrate on and change now?

My Breakthrough Area

Source completewellbeing.com

List the most recurrent challenges you are dealing with on a daily basis in this area of your life to concentrate on it now.

Challenges	How do they make you think, feel, behave, eat, and sleep?

"Winners never quit, and quitters never win."

Vince Lombardi

Describe in writing the area of life that you are not living up to, where things are not working out the way you want them to.

Area where you are defensive, where you are obsessed by your thoughts and react to your emotions in a limiting way.

Be brutally honest with yourself and consider:

- What is stopping you from achieving what you want?
- If you don't do anything about it now and if you don't change your pattern (habit), what does it cost you?
- What would happen if you didn't break through after reading this book and practising the learning? What is the ultimate cost?
- What would happen if you did break through after reading this book and practice the learning?

"A problem well stated, is a problem half solved."

Charles Kettering

On a scale of 1 to 10 (1 interested and 10 will do whatever it takes), how much do you want it? _____

If the answer is below 10, you are not COMMITTED; you will not solve this issue. Only if you are willing 100 per cent to do whatever it takes will you succeed.

What is stopping you?	Ultimate costs	Breakthrough gains

I encourage you to have a breakthrough practice notebook, where you will replicate the exercises and use as much space as necessary. Note down the date and time for each work you do.

Tree of Life

On each leaf, think of how you could tackle each challenge by changing the way you think about it. What solutions can you think of? How can you solve it? What would you do differently?

Solution Tree

"There are 3 steps to wealth:
1. Wake up
2. Choose your game
3. Play to win."

Christopher Howard

My Goals for Change

Write down three to five goals you want to achieve in the area of your life that needs your full attention now, and that you have just identified.

Your goals should be written in the **present tense**, as if they are already achieved, Now.

Make each goal measurable and compelling: what do you see, hear, taste, smell, touch, and feel. What do you say to yourself? What is your achievement sensory evidence?

_____
_____
_____
_____
_____
_____
_____
_____
_____
_____

Mental Visualisation

Close your eyes and consider your commitment to the above goals. Rise up in the sky, high up; imagine being an eagle; fly high and float above the present moment, look down at now with the eyes of the observer (eagle), notice your past (however it presents to you) and your future (however it appears). Rise up so you are higher than everything. Everything is so small below, and you see your goals in purple (the colour of imagination). You are in a place of pure creation; visualise the person you want to be. The person who broke through his/her limitations, and achieved the set goals SEE IT, HEAR IT, SMELL IT, TASTE

IT, TOUCH IT, FEEL IT AND BREATHE IT. You know you CAN do it. When you have felt an intense motivation invading you from top to bottom, and a great feeling of happiness, you can slowly open your eyes.

Repeat this visualisation daily, your crew will prepare all the resources you need to make it happen and you will attract the right opportunities.

Mind Management and Mind-Body Connection

As communication begins in our mind; the information received in our brain and body will be interpreted as an internal representation (thought or meaning given to the information received) and create a unique subjective reality that is ours.

We use words, a voice quality, and body language that describe our internal state and thoughts. Then, we communicate and project it to others. The external information is reconfigured as an internal representation (thought), which is linked to an internal state (emotional, physical, and mental state). Science demonstrated that the thought triggers an emotion and immediate reaction physiologically through a combination of chemicals released by every cell in our body to the entire nervous system. We end up producing a certain behaviour that will affect our results and performance (explanatory charts coming up in the next pages).

The problem with whatever you think is that you project it automatically.

What happens if your thought was negative? As in when you extrapolate what is affecting your life at the present moment with how it is going to impact your future, playing mainly unpleasant scenarios of what might happen, and you will narratively speak to yourself to prove this thought. Example: "Oh my God, I will lose my job, what am I going to do?" You see yourself with all the debts that may occur, your inner dialogue spices up, you then click a fear mechanism that will drag anxiety etc., and you enter a stuck process, trapped in your own mental jail.

What do you say to yourself regularly?

- Do you say to yourself that I hope I won't blow this conversation (or meeting, or relationship, or diet . . .) like I did last time?
- Or when you are communicating with your children and you say to yourself that I won't get angry like last time?
- Or are you saying to yourself that I hope I will be happy?
- What thoughts or internal dialogue do you hold in your mind at the beginning of each process?

We have thousands of thoughts a day, which are not all positive. You cannot control every single thought that pops up in your head, but what you CAN DO is pay attention to what you are thinking and GAIN CONTROL over your reactions to certain thoughts. Our thinking errors become the norm when we keep thinking them for a period of time and they obsess us. Frustration and anxiety increase until you decide to deal with those burdening thoughts that you blow out of proportion.

In my case, this learning helped me understand that if I utilise this function consciously, I will gain control and empower myself to choose the way I want to perceive and act in the world to produce the results I most desire. I stopped labelling an experience as being the reality. I would step back and, through silence within, I would try to remember and get more information from my unconscious mind before I decide or choose anything.

THE SECOND STEP 119

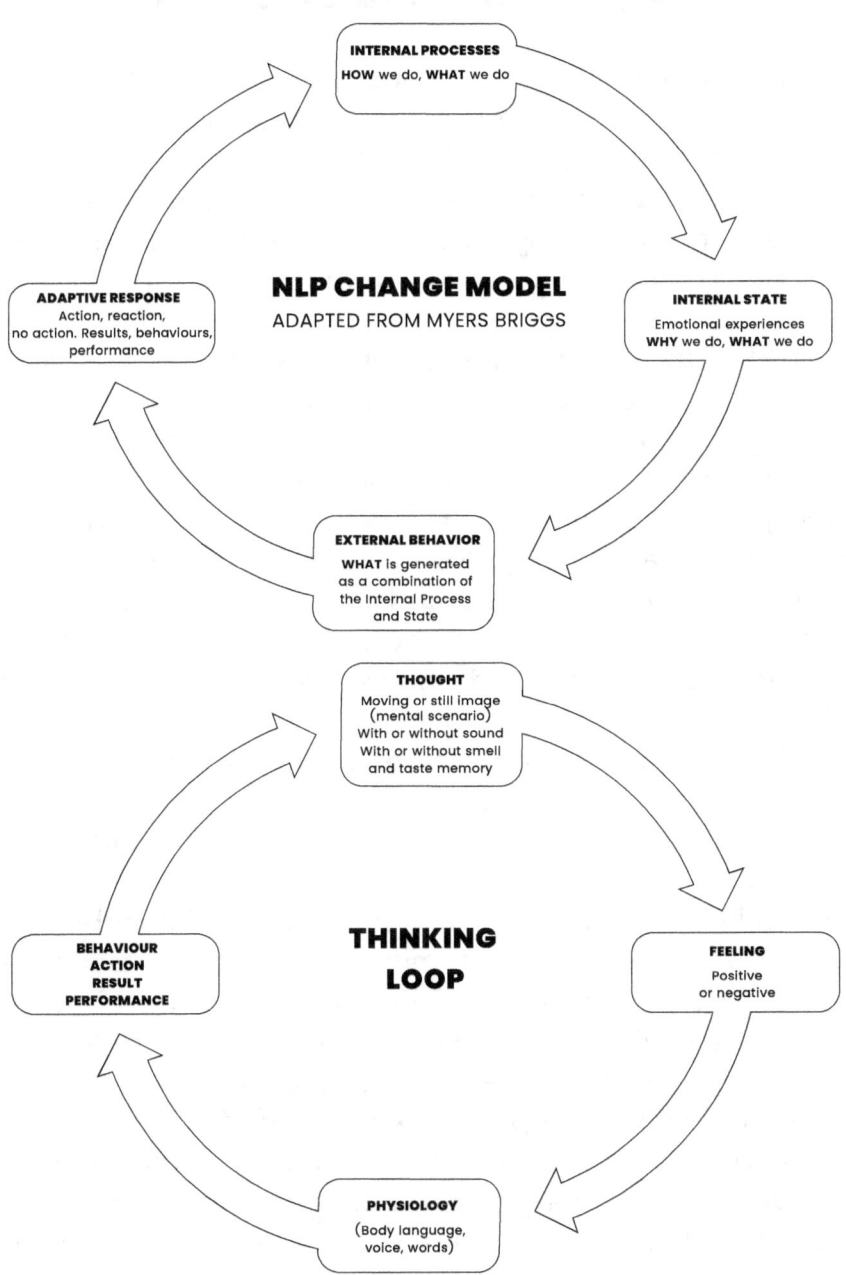

Mind performance charts explanation

- A negative thought provokes a negative feeling and physiological response, and ends up with negative behaviour, action, result and low performance.
- A positive thought leads to a positive feeling and physiological response, and ends up with a positive behaviour, action, result, and optimal performance.

As per Bell's theorem, the observer always and intimately affects the observed. In a quantum mechanical universe (meaning how the universe works at a smaller scale than atoms, and how particles that make up atoms work and move), there is no locality of information. Our current understanding of time, space, matter, and energy lose all of their meaning. There is no difference between here and there, which underlines the interconnectedness to everything in the universe. There is no difference between you and what you see outside of you.

"The world is a reflection of your consciousness."

Carl Jung

On the other hand, if we look at neuroscientist Karl Pribram and physicist David Bohm's holonomic brain theory, it describes the brain as holographic storage of memory. When you look at a hologram, the whole is in the part and the part is in the whole. All the information necessary to create the entire hologram is contained within the piece. Like a seed in an apple, all the information about the apple tree is contained in the seed. Then you have the apple that grows on the tree and you have a new seed, and within each new seed, all the information required to create the tree again. According to Karl Pribram, human memory storage works the same way. The whole is in the part and the part is in the whole.

Dr. Deepak Chopra, author of the book *Quantum Healing*, talks about human memory contained through the entire body. Every single cell in our body listens to everything we are thinking, the words we use, the sounds in our head, as well as the pictures in our mind, and it feels our feelings. All this happens simultaneously, and all of it is affecting our behaviour, our actions, our results and the quality of our performance.

This is the scientific proof of the mind-body connection. We are suggestible beings and our body reacts to our mind's thoughts.

In quantum reality, our internal world equals our external world. We can't look at something without affecting it and changing it in some way. So, the world changes based upon who is observing it. The observer and the observed are interconnected. And as there is no locality of interconnection, there is no difference between you and what appears outside of you. In other words, whenever you think and whatever you think you are, you are much more than that. Whatever you think puts boundary conditions on the unlimitedness that is you and within you. You have the entire universe's resources.

All that exists in the external world is pure data with no intrinsic meaning. We give meaning to experience. Each interpretation is unique to the individual that experiences it. That meaning will determine your reality and will affect your internal state, behaviour, and results. In other words, until you look at the problem and measure it, the problem doesn't exist. It is your reality, not the reality.

> **"Your body hears everything your mind says.
> Speak kind words."**
>
> Dr. Deepak Chopra

Pay attention to how you speak to yourself; if you only use diminishing, sabotaging and unkind language, you are definitely planning to fail and be unhappy. Use positive affirmations and kind words when you speak to yourself; you will certainly succeed and achieve greater results.

> **"Perception is projection."**
>
> Carl Jung

This theme helped me a lot to become aware and conscious that I can't see anything outside of me which isn't me. The world around me is a reflection of me, of my consciousness. Whatever I thought, I would project on others and on the environment around me. This theme clarified communication misunderstandings and judgments I used to hold.

I use this theme in all my teaching.
If you look outside you and you see poor physical health, that's you.
If you look outside you and you see unhappiness, that's you.
If you look outside you and you see conflict, that's you.
On the other hand, if you see great relationships, that's you as well.
If you see justice, that's you.
Everything is a reflection of your consciousness. You can't hide your thoughts as, unconsciously, you extrapolate them.

> Whenever you are obsessed by any thoughts (your demons) that prevent you from living happy and make you think that you have no choice, write them down and then share them with the person you trust the most. A weight will be lifted off your shoulders. Pay attention to them with the eyes of the observer, the HERO, and not of the victim.

A weak mind perceives a situation as a problem.
A thought-controlled mind perceives a situation as a challenge.
A herculean mind (adopting Hercules' great strength and courage) turns a situation into an opportunity.

Thinking Process and Information Filtering System

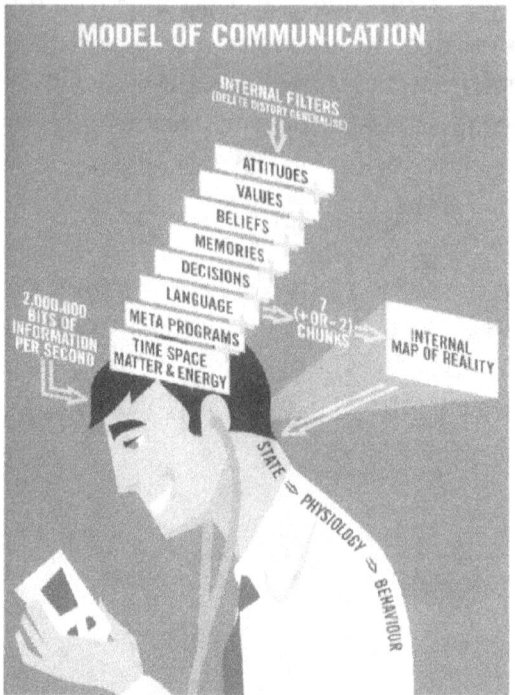

Source: CHC Fast Track To Success

Internal filters,
YOUR hidden rule book

Hungarian biologist Mihaly Csikszentmihalyi in his book *Flow, the psychology of optimal experience*, says that we are bombarded each second by approximately two million bits of information that we take in via our five senses. We cannot possibly be aware of all the information we receive; our nervous system would go insane. The reticular activating system located at the base of our brain is responsible for a number of functions, out of which one is consciously FILTERING the information and sorting it out to make it manageable. After receiving an external event through the senses, the mind and the body interpret and then give it a meaning by running it through the internal processing system. This combines the biological filters of the Reticular Activating System (RAS) with other more psychologically based internal filters that create a unique subjective reality for each individual. Interrupting and taking charge of these internal filters is key to mental, emotional, and behavioural mastery.

Those internal filters, formed and maintained by the unconscious mind, tell the RAS what information to sort out, those things that confirm your long-held beliefs and expectations (the hidden rule book).

Sometimes, you use this process in a way that robs you of options and power. Now you can consciously utilise this function to empower yourself by choosing the way you want to see and act in the world in order to produce the results you most desire.

Out of the two million bits of information, we process consciously seven plus or minus two chunks, which is about 134 bits of information; the rest will be stored unconsciously. For this to happen, as per Noam Chomsky's 1957 PhD thesis, *Transformational Grammar*, he said that we delete, distort, and generalise information by which we create our "reality."

Internal filters determine what we focus on, look for, sort, and what is left out of our experience of reality.

Internal filters are created by:

- Upbringing
- Environment
- Significant Emotional Experiences (SEE); those impactful experiences that remain imprinted in our memory "blueprints."

People assume their "reality" reflects an absolute "truth." Having minds "set" already in a certain way doesn't allow room for change or the expansion of the sphere of influence. How can you expect to get more out of life if you think and act in the same way you and possibly your ancestors always have? You can change your mindset and internal filters, and thereby your outcomes.

Internal filters include values, beliefs, attitudes, memories, decisions, language, meta programmes, time, space, matter, and energy.

If we consider the world of a child born in war and another child born in a peaceful country, do they live in different worlds? Without a doubt. What determines the world they live in?

Their focus.

By changing the toxic country, city, home, work, and people, you will heal, grow, and enhance your quality of life. I am a great example of environment evaluation and change.

Or other examples: What was important to you last year might not be important to you now. What you are missing in your life at the moment becomes of high importance and you constantly think about it until you obtain it.

Information Filtering System

1. **Deletion:** A large amount of incoming data is left out to avoid sensory overload. You selectively pay attention to certain aspects of experience based

on your internal filters. Because you get what you focus on and can't experience what you delete, the experience of life is largely dependent upon what information you are taking out at any given moment. So, how can you believe that the meaning you gave to an experience is reality when most of the information you received is removed? We cannot experience what we erase.

2. **Distortion:** A person's judgment consists of creating, imagining, and interpreting a set of data. Although people may experience the same event, they will interpret it differently. Each will base his description on his own model of the world. "My husband didn't say good morning to me today: he must be angry with me!" is an interpretation of behaviours, while perhaps he had other things going on in his mind. Sometimes we arbitrarily construe reality and we end up distorting its meaning, seeing things that do not exist.

3. **Generalisation:** Your unconscious mind organises information as an overall picture. This can benefit or limit you because generalisations make up belief systems and may be based on your personal experience (social, cultural, gender, age, ethnicity, religion, or occupation) and this eliminates choice and disempowers you in many ways. Example: "I could never reach this," "You always misunderstand what I say," "I will never be good at this," "My boss never gives me positive feedback," "I can't make a lot of money and be happy . . . "

Your Thinking Map Components

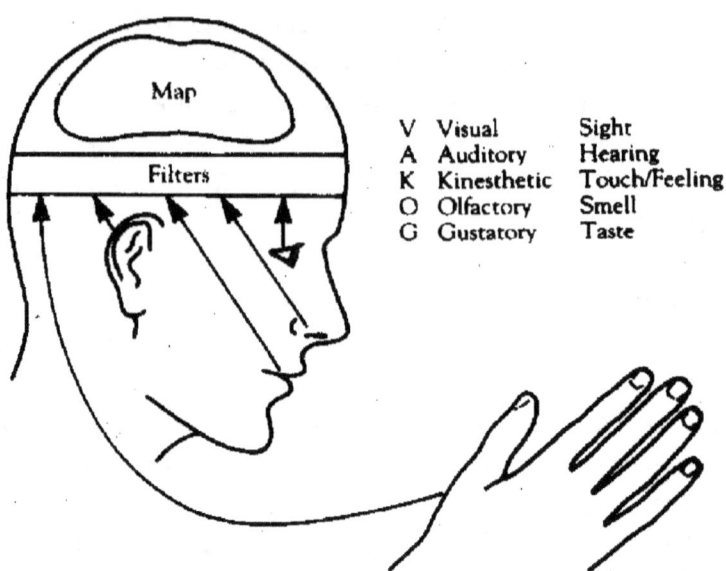

V   Visual   Sight
A   Auditory   Hearing
K   Kinesthetic   Touch/Feeling
O   Olfactory   Smell
G   Gustatory   Taste

Representational Systems

V	Ve	Visual External	What you see outside you
	Vi	Visual Internal	What you see in your mind
A	Ae	Auditory External	External sounds you hear
	Ai	Auditory Internal	Internal sounds of other people' voices in your head
	Ad	Auditory Digital	Self-talk, your inner voice
K	Ke	Kinesthetic	External tactile sensations, touch
	Ki	Kinesthetic	Emotions/Feelings
		Gustatory & Olfactory	External sense and internal memory

Your Thinking Strategy Exercise

Discover how you think, how your thought kicks in, and where it ends up.

Some people see the world, others hear it or feel it. These *unconscious mental maps* are guides that help you make decisions on how to respond to whatever is going on around you. These thinking modes are the most natural and unconscious.

Write a NUMBER next to EACH of the following statements using the below indicators:

    4 (Describing you 100 per cent)
    3 (Describing you 75 per cent)
    2 (Describing you 50 per cent)
    1 (Least descriptive of you, 25 per cent)

You can only use each number once. Read and answer what comes first to your mind naturally and not thinking over it, as you want to discover how you think unconsciously and not consciously.

Example:
1. I make important decisions based on:
 ____4____ Gut level feelings
 ____1____ Which way it sounds the best to me
 ____3____ What looks best to me
 ____2____ Review and study of the issues.

Your turn now.

1. I make important decisions based on:
 _____ Gut level feelings
 _____ Which way it sounds the best to me

_____ What looks best to me
_____ Review and study of the issues.

2. **During an argument, I am most likely to be influenced by:**
_____ The other person's tone of voice
_____ Whether or not I can see the other person's point of view
_____ The logic of the other person's argument
_____ Whether or not I am in touch with the other person's feelings.

3. **I most easily communicate what is going on with me by:**
_____ The way I dress and look
_____ The feelings I share
_____ The words I choose
_____ The tonality of my voice.

4. **It is easier for me to:**
_____ Find the ideal volume on TV
_____ Select the most relevant point in a subject
_____ Select the most comfortable clothes
_____ Select attractive colour combinations.

5. **I am**
_____ I am very sensitive to the sounds of my surroundings
_____ I like making sense of new facts and information
_____ I am very sensitive to the quality of the fabric on my body
_____ I have a very strong response to colours and to the way a room looks.

6. **My strength lies in my capacity of:**
_____ Listening
_____ Understanding the information

_____ Being sensitive to others' emotions
_____ See what needs to be done.

7. I find a presentation interesting if:
_____ I like the speaker and feel emotions
_____ The speaker uses visuals
_____ What the speaker says is based on facts and figures
_____ The speaker has a good voice tonality and rhythm to reinforce his or her message.

8. When I am given a task, I can accomplish it if:
_____ I can visualise it
_____ I can feel it
_____ I can understand it
_____ I listened properly.

9. In social situations
_____ I tend to forget names but remember people's faces
_____ I tend to remember what was done, not what was seen or talked about
_____ I tend to forget faces but remember individuals names
_____ I usually remember the details and facts of what had happened.

10. In communication
_____ I appreciate being in physical contact and close to people
_____ I repeat things to myself and enjoy talking in detail
_____ I enjoy listening but can't wait to talk
_____ I use gestures when speaking, listen poorly, and get bored with too much detail.

132 HAPPYDEMIC

Step One: Copy your answers from the previous pages vertically:

Example:
1.   4   K
       1   A
       3   V
       2   Ad

1. _____ K
    _____ A
    _____ V
    _____ Ad

2. _____ A
    _____ V
    _____ Ad
    _____ K

3. _____ V
    _____ K
    _____ Ad
    _____ A

4. _____ A
    _____ Ad
    _____ K
    _____ V

5. _____ A
    _____ Ad
    _____ K
    _____ V

6. _____ A
    _____ Ad
    _____ K
    _____ V

7. _____ K
    _____ V
    _____ Ad
    _____ A

8. _____ V
    _____ K
    _____ Ad
    _____ A

9. _____ V
    _____ K
    _____ A
    _____ Ad

10. _____ K
     _____ Ad
     _____ A
     _____ V

Step Two: Copy the number associated with each letter horizontally. Sum-up the numbers by column. The total of the four columns should be 100.

		V	A	K	Ad
Based on above example:		3	1	4	2
	1				
	2				
	3				
	4				
	5				
	6				
	7				
	8				
	9				
	10	↓	↓	↓	↓
Total of four columns = 100		+	+	+	+

The highest score in the total column will give you your preferred thinking mode. Write the letter (or letters, a synesthesia of two letters with the same total, meaning that several senses kick in simultaneously) in the circle.

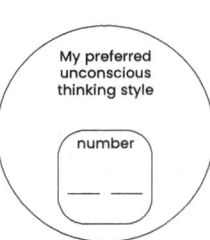

My preferred unconscious thinking style

number

_ _ _

My Thinking Strategy:
Letter with highest score—next closer—next closer—lowest score

---

Example: V-K-A-Ad, you start a thought by seeing, afterwards you feel and need to experience it, then you talk about it, and you end your thinking process by analysing it.

There is so much we can cover regarding this topic, I am only giving you an overview to understand how you think and what your thoughts are composed of.

Visual thinker: Interested by HOW things look. Memorises and understands by illustration (internal and external images), and is less distracted by noise. Is usually bored by long verbal instructions. Is very sensitive to body language, appearance of people and things. Usually confident, well groomed, organised, speaks fast and is good with directions. Verbal vocabulary is composed of: *See, show, colour, shape, size, picture, clear, look, view, perceive, illustrate, highlight, focus, reflect, watch, perspective, appear, imagine, observe, etc.*

Auditory thinker: Loves gathering information, learns by listening, and likes to talk. Easily distracted by noise, and good at repeating things back. Is very sensible to the tone of voice and the choice of words. Interested in WHAT is said and how it sounds. Vocabulary composed of: *Hear, ask, listen, sound, harmonise, tune in/out, be all ears, silence, tell, announce, dialogue, speak, etc.*

Auditory digital thinker: High self-talk. Memorises by steps and procedures. Very analytical, logical, and has to make sense of the information received. Need facts. Interested in WHAT is said in an organised manner and the information has to make sense. A mind before a heart. Vocabulary composed of: *Sense, understand, think, process, consider, know, question, logic, statistically, fact, etc.*

Kinesthetic thinker: Responds and needs close physical distance with people. Memorises by doing, trying, testing, and experiencing. Likes to touch and sense the environment. A feeler, a heart before mind. Interested if it feels right, and how it's experienced. Vocabulary composed of: *Emotions, sensations with touch, grasp, experience, etc.*

Note: Your thinking strategy may change with time based on your career position, your needs at that moment, and your personal evolution.

The Power of Focus

We are given the most wonderful device for creating behaviour, the best creation in the universe's history, and you have it at your disposal: The human nervous system that holds more neurological connections than all the stars in the sky. What are you doing with it?

We are in charge of our mind, therefore, we are in charge of the results it produces.

Imagine your mind as being a computer. If you go on your search engine and type the word "unhappy," what is going to come up on your screen (conscious)? You will get all the websites (memories, thoughts, and experiences) from your past and you might mistake that for being all that there is. But there is a WHOLE lot more out there. In life, we get what we look for depending on where we focus. Imagine you were in the dark room of life; in one corner there is unhappiness, in the other corner there is happiness, above there are opportunities, below there are limitations . . . If you look at the world, they all exist, isn't it? They are available somewhere. How is it that you only experience one and not the other? What becomes your experience of life is where you focus your flashlight on (consciously), your 134 bits of information. We live in a universe of pure abundance and potentiality. Wake up and tap into it, allow your wants and needs to flow to you.

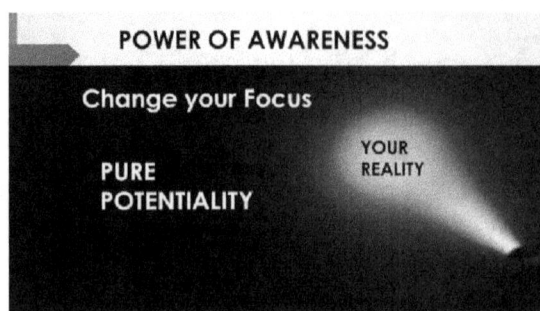

What is lit by your flashlight is your reality, and all the black around is pure potentiality, and THE reality.

Source: tkthorne.com

Change your focus

Expand your awareness from foveal (2 to 10 degrees), to peripheral vision (180 degrees), and maximise your opportunities attraction by opening up to a full 360 degrees.

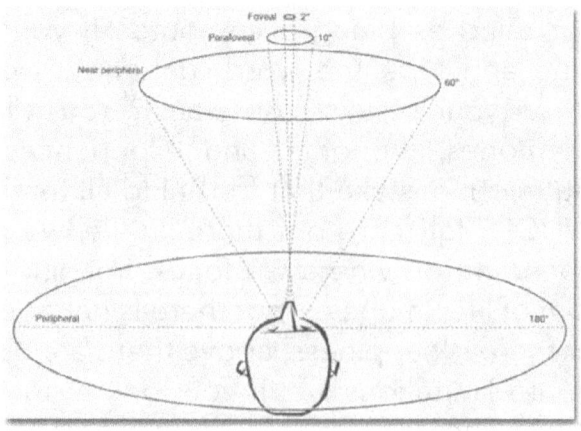

Source: v360.ie

Our focus determines the world we live in. Your map of reality is a representation, it is not the territory. Change your experience by substituting the explanation and the meaning you gave it.

"Through pain, there's GAIN."

Larissa Redaelli

Wake up, increase your awareness of who you are, what you want to become and listen to your unconscious messages. Build rapport with your crew and observe your results. Where you were yesterday and where do you stand today compared to where you want to be? Stop, think, plan, and do something about it NOW instead of complaining and finding excuses to justify your actions. Always be a BETTER VERSION of yourself. The key to create your future is in your hands. It's all about self-leadership and regaining control of your thoughts, emotions, and actions.

**"The happiness of your life
Depends on the quality of your thoughts."**

Marcus Aurelius

Values

These are our key motivators. What we are driven by, that means soooo much to us.

Sociologist Dr. Morris Massey speaks about three key development stages where we build our values:

1. **Imprint period** (age 0-7), in which we function like a sponge; we soak in values and beliefs from our parents,

our environment, our religion, our school, media, economics, and geography that will affect our personality and what we look for in life. We have this blueprint embedded in us. Thoughts that conditioned us, and unless we have significant emotional events that shift our personality, grow up finding positive and empowering role models or change the interpretation of our limiting thoughts, we tend to stay as we are.

2. **Modelling period** (age 7-14), in which we look up to a hero or role model to become similar to or not be assimilated to.

3. **Socialisation period** (age 14-21), which defines who we hang out with. The good and bad group of friends.

William James, the Father of American psychology, adds on to Dr. Massey's work: the **business persona** work ethic (age 21-30). This considers our first work experience and environment and its impact on us, together with other work experiences.

> "Who you are today is who you modelled in your imprint period,
> Who you become is who you model.
> Expand your model of the world."
>
> Dr. Morris Massey

I was very lucky, I had the best first work experience; it was a great second school with a leader figure who gave me all the growth opportunities even though he was a tough old-school leader. This experience was a great boost to my self-esteem and work motivation. It was indeed the start of a successful career path.

> **"In life, we don't get what we want,
> we get what we expect."**
>
> Dennis Waitley

We need to really understand what makes up our personality and drives us in our lives. I will talk about values, not our identity values, but the ones you apply in your daily life in all fields unconsciously. Becoming conscious of what is important to us in order to direct our actions and energy towards what we want or fill what is missing in our life. If things aren't working the way you want, I would first question my values. I will explain how you can elicit your surface and deeper unconscious values, put them in a hierarchy of importance to focus on achieving them, analyse where you stand today, where you want to be and how you can reach there. How will you align your desires and honour your innermost callings?

Values are broad concepts that guide our decisions in life. They determine what is important to us, what has value in our life, career, relationship, and health . . . They are the foundation of our character and the triggers to our fulfilment. The higher the calling, the more we become passionate, and will put all the necessary energy, resources, and focus to accomplish it.

- They can be detected by what we are attracted to, or repulsed by, what we perceive to be missing in our life, and by our actions.
- They provide upfront motivation, determine how we spend our time and act upon in our world.

Examples:
- An individual whose top value is wealth will invest time and effort in that area. Their experience in life will reflect

that focus. If some of those same individuals do not also value honesty, then their route to wealth would be very different from others who highly value both wealth and honesty.
- A child brought up in Lebanon has happiness values that are different from a child who grew up in Switzerland.
- Having a part of you that wants commitment and another part that wants autonomy.
- If you are missing recognition and feedback at work, two important values for you, your motivation will be affected as well as your happiness and performance.

We may not like something we do but if we believe it is important, we will still do it. We need to understand our values system functioning to shift our results by becoming aware of our conscious and unconscious callings, to align them congruently towards our goals, CONSCIOUSLY. Often, we quit our jobs because we don't share the same values as our managers or the company we work for. The same applies to a relationship.

Recognising, reprioritising, and aligning conscious and unconscious values are major steps towards focusing and getting what we truly want, ignoring what's not important.

Motivation Direction

Motivation within values can be conflicting as per Herzberg's theory of gain of pleasure and avoidance of pain:

- **Motivated to move towards what we want:** Something that gives us pleasure or a reward of some kind, recognised by the use of direct and positive language, "I want . . ." Focused on the objective, excited, and energised by goals. Motivated to have, get, gain, achieve, include.

- **Motivated away from problems and avoiding pain:** Notices what should be avoided and gotten rid of. Motivation triggered when there is a problem to be solved or to move away from. Energised by threats, and deadlines to take action. It's an escape from pain and a punishment motivation. Good at troubleshooting, and pinpointing obstacles during planning, picks up on what is or could be going wrong.

  Have trouble maintaining focus on goals, easily distracted by, and compelled to respond to negative situations. Will drop everything to fix something. Concentrated on treating crises.

  Difficulty in managing priorities.

  "I don't want . . ." "I must or I should . . ." "I have to . . . better, more, or less . . ." This is a yo-yo effort in motivation as when you achieve it, your motivation falls off, then you struggle until you reach . . . and when you do, your motivation drops again.

Motivation Source

- **Intrinsic motivation:** When we satisfy our core values, self-motivation comes from within, passion, professionalism, self-confidence. . .
- **Extrinsic motivation:** An external factor is responsible for our motivation, a reward, someone's feedback or punishment.

Think about it. Do you move towards the things that you want or away from the things that you don't want to see happening? There is no right or wrong way; it varies depending on the situation, yet moving towards achieving drives you positively and clearly towards your goal. On the one hand, moving away from pain drives you with more effort, negative feelings and is one of the reasons why we don't achieve what we want. Moreover we end up experiencing pain. On the other hand, motivation that emanates from you is more powerful than expecting or counting on external factors to motivate you.

Values Source

Friends, family, environment, media, religion, school, geography.

There are **surface values** (at the surface of our unconscious mind) and **core values** (**innermost underlying unconscious drivers** that are profoundly rooted). To dig deeper, you need to keep asking yourself what is important to you about something, and keep repeating the process to unravel more. What do you want to achieve? What's important to you about that?

Think of something you like doing and write it down.
_____

Why do you like doing it?
_____

What is important to you about doing that?
_____
_____

Career Values Elicitation Example

To make the values elicitation technique in all areas of your life easier to grasp, I will teach you how to extract your career values, as most of us relate to it with less mental blockages and resistance.

To start the elicitation, you need to ask yourself the below question in the exact wording, since, if you change it, the end result isn't the same.

Ask yourself:

What is important to me about my job/career?

What's important to me about that?

Keep on going up to as many values as you can think of. Write all that comes to your mind; the first things that come out are the surface conscious values. You will arrive at a point where consciously you can't think of anything anymore. Read all the values you wrote and ask yourself again:

What else is important to me about my job/career?

Push yourself. This is the first step in delving into the unconscious values. You need to push yourself at least twice to go deeper into your unconscious mind. You will notice that values are nominalisations (use of a verb, adjective or adverb as a noun). For example: "positive people," or "communication" or "decision." Values are composed of few words and not sentences.

Surface values

- Job satisfaction.
- Recognition.
- Teamwork.
- Remuneration.
- Positive working environment.

***First blank:* answers from unconscious mind**
- Positive people.
- Good leaders and managers.
- Learning.

***Second blank:* deeper unconscious level**
- Happiness.
- Work-life balance.
- Time management.
- Promotion.

You need to organise your values by order of significance, from the most important without which you wouldn't do this job, to the least important.

Values Hierarchy
1- Happiness
2- Work-life balance
3- Promotion
4- Positive working environment
5- Good leaders and managers
6- Learning
7- Remuneration
8- Job Satisfaction
9- Recognition
10- Promotion
11- Time management
12- Teamwork

As I look at the hierarchy, does it really reflect my reality in the job at the moment? What is not working? What is missing? If I am not happy and am not having a work-life balance, I notice that these two values weren't in my conscious top five values. I need to put them at the top of my priorities in order to focus on them consciously, to turn them into an urge calling, make the shift, and produce change.

Another way to understand how we are so unaware of our values is to notice that in my top hierarchy, deep unconscious callings are there and I have become aware of their importance. The deeper you go, the more unconscious values appear to your conscious, and the more you can influence your results by changing your focus and destiny path.

Self-motivation within your values

How are you driven within your values? Are you positively driven towards achieving your goal (gain of pleasure) or away from pain?

The question we ask to discover our motivation direction is:

Why is (value) important to me?

Example: Why is **happiness** important to me? Write the answer and look at the words you used.

If you are doing the values elicitation with other people, listen actively to what is being said.

There are three flags that will highlight an away-from motivation:

1. Words that relate to comparison: more, less, words ending with "er" (happier), or "est" (best)
2. Necessity words: have to, should do, must do . . .
3. Negation words: not, no.

Why is happiness important to me?
It is my ultimate goal; whatever I do or think, I keep happiness in mind. If I am not happy I cannot perform nor achieve. Being happy makes my family and environment happier. When unhappy, I am confused, I can't think clearly. I feel stuck and unhealthy. My mind is worried about being unhappy. My inner voice warns me all the time to be careful, to make sure I am contented.

If you look at my reply on an average, do you think I am positively driven or negatively driven towards happiness? What feeling does it give you? Do I use more sentences with away from signals or more positively driven words? In this example, I am definitely negatively driven, and to achieve happiness, I am exhausted with the focus on what I don't want to see happening. Yet, what am I producing? Unhappiness for sure.

I definitely need to change my inner language and use happiness speech to direct my thoughts and emotions towards happy achievements.

It's your turn for action now

Take a moment to elicit your career/job values and follow the step-by-step process. Choose a quiet place where you feel safe and focused. Keep all distractions away.

The same process can be used to elicit values in a different context or any other area of your life: love values, relationship values, spiritual values, health values, personal growth values, decision-making values, buying values, etc.

My Career Values Elicitation

Ask yourself.
1. What is important to me about my career, my job?
2. What is important to me about that?
3. What else is important to me about my career, my job?

_____
_____
_____
_____
_____
_____
_____
_____
_____
_____

Values Hierarchy	**Motivation Direction**
What is the most important to me without which I won't do this job? What is less, to the least important?	**Why is ... (value) important to me?** Pleasure motivation, **Towards** (T); Pain motivation, **Away From** (A/F)

As you look at your job values, ask yourself what is not working or missing at the moment in your job? Where are you today? Where do you need to focus your flashlight? How can you do that? You will notice that you aren't focusing on what is really important to you at the deep unconscious level. The moment you become aware of it, you will definitely start focusing on it and you will see the change happening.

Example: When I wasn't pregnant, nor did I plan for it, I used to go to the shopping malls and definitely not see any baby shop, nor notice pregnant women, pushchairs, etc., it wasn't important to me nor was it in my focus. The moment I got pregnant, I only saw pregnant women, baby accessories, and room decorations, etc., it became so important to me, a top value in the hierarchy of my pregnancy context.

Beliefs

Beliefs are generalisations about life, the world, and our ability to act. They are convictions and acceptance of statements by what is held to be true for us (our truths). They often form the boundary conditions of our thinking and create limiting beliefs depending on how much we are willing to trust is possible.

When you acknowledge your limiting beliefs as a means to set you free and transform them into empowering beliefs, you can fulfill your highest potential.

Example: If someone believes, he can learn anything that he puts his mind to regardless of age, then his experience of life is going to be different from someone else who believes he is too experienced and can't possibly learn more than he knows.

"Small possibility thinking gives small results."

"Our beliefs about WHO WE ARE and
WHAT WE CAN BE,
Determine WHO WE WILL BE."

Tony Robbins

"Courage is the first of human qualities, because it is the quality which guarantees all others."

Winston Churchill

"Your Past doesn't equal to your Future."

Tony Robbins

"Whether you think you CAN or you can't,
Either way YOU ARE RIGHT!"

Henry Ford

If you believe that you can succeed and you put your mind to it, you will succeed.

If you believe you are shy, you also put your mind to it; all you will do is prove to your own self that you are right by putting yourself down, and staying in the background. Any belief formed with a lack of ability to do, be, or have something you want, is a limiting belief.

Beliefs should help you grow in life and not paralyse you. Anything that stops you from progressing needs to go now. We are not born with limiting beliefs; we acquired them along the way, from something someone said or did to us or something we heard. You held onto these beliefs, yet you can choose to get rid of them as they don't benefit you. Focus on your strengths and manage your weaknesses.

"Believe and act as if it were **IMPOSSIBLE** to FAIL."

Charles Kettering

"Whatever the mind can conceive and believe, it can achieve."

Napoleon Hill

The Power of Beliefs Exercise

What beliefs do you hold about yourself?

EMPOWERING Beliefs	Limiting Beliefs	Questions To Ask Yourself
Your strengths and qualities Help you progress, and achieve Happy	Your weaknesses and limitations Block you Can't be, do, or have Unhappy	• How does this belief benefit you? • If it doesn't benefit you, why are you holding on to it? (What is your secondary gain?)
A strong team player		I succeed in my work being in a team; it's all about WE. Sharing and winning together motivate me.

	Shy	I don't have to make any effort in socialising with people. I have nothing interesting to share. I don't want to be rejected so I hang on to my comfort zone.
Life is beautiful		
	Am not worthy	Do everything to prove myself right, bad self-talk.
	Work hard	
Work smart		
	Am not good enough	
Faith		

"About the past . . .
The way I see it, you can either run from it, or learn from it."

Rafiki to Simba in *The Lion King*

Self-confidence: It is the most attractive quality a person can have. How can people see how great you are if you don't see it yourself?

Self-awareness: Notice when you have a limiting belief. When you become aware of it, you gain power over it, and this gives you the ability to control it before it controls you. Persistence is the key; if it doesn't work the first time keep doing, keep going, and keep growing.

Limiting Beliefs Exercise

1. Look at your limitations. Which is the most disturbing one you hold about yourself that blocks you, jeopardises your results and makes you feel stuck?
2. How is that a problem? What is stopping you from being, doing, or having? (Costs)
3. How can you overcome this? What do you want to be, do, or have instead? (Gains)
4. How will you achieve change? What actions will you take NOW?
5. What resources will you need? Resources as in: constructive thoughts and feelings, behaviours, beneficial habits, actions, effective time management, qualities, people (Who can help you?), attitude, books, research . . .
6. By when will you time this change? How often will you follow up on your improvements and review the time frame when necessary? (Agenda management: For example, the beginning of the week, every two weeks, or at the end of each month . . .)

The most disturbing and limiting belief I hold about myself.

Example: Procrastination.

I want instead: Motivation, fuel to drive forward.

Your turn.
_____
_____

Costs	Gains	Actions Rectification strategies	Resources	Agenda Management
• Low results • Lack of energy • Others' judgement etc.	• Increase in results • Energy to drive • Recognition etc.	• Focus • Remove distractions • Find interest • Clear my mind etc.	• Believe in me • Positive attitude • Movement • Ask help from etc.	• Start: today • Ongoing • Follow up on my improvements and challenges, every Sunday evening

"A goal without a deadline is just a dream;
Turn your dreams into goals."

Inspired by Antoine de Saint-Exupéry

My DAILY EMPOWERING BELIEFS Diary

:)

Every morning, write three empowering beliefs, qualities, or strengths that describe you: professional, helpful, funny, lovable, humble, caring . . .

Stand in front of a mirror and take a superhero pose. Straight back, lengthen your neck as if your head is pulled by a string from the ceiling, open your chest, look in front of you, smile, and say it out loud at least three times; notice your feelings and anchor them when they are intense.

> "You don't have to be great to start,
> but, you have to start to be great."
>
> Zig Ziglar

Other Internal Filters

Attitudes

A Frame of Mind: Attitudes are abstract ideas coming from clusters of beliefs and values around a given subject. The glasses through which you see the world, colourful or black. They are often hard to pinpoint and their effect is insidious. They can distort your perspective positively or negatively and subsequently determine what you achieve in life. Sometimes, they stand between you and the outcomes you want.

In my opinion, attitude is the most important projection of you. It is your success or your failure, your friend or your enemy.

Example: A person who has a positive attitude towards work and sees any given feedback as growth will have a different experience to someone with a negative attitude, who sees feedback as criticism and takes it personally.

Memories

Memories filter your current experience of reality. They are often the rationale for keeping a belief whether for your good or not. Because the brain tends to categorise events in relation to previous experiences, both the present and the future are evaluated or anticipated based on the meaning given to the past event.

Memories are only stored as selected snapshots of a multidimensional event that took place and kept as a belief categorised on the meaning you gave that past event.

Example: An old photograph of you when you were a child looking unhappy. The memory itself may be faded or even forgotten, but is stored at the unconscious level. However, the meaning of the event is stored neurologically in such a way that a similar event stimulates the old associations and gives the same or similar meaning to the "new" event. Faded memories often direct what actions people choose to take, making their behaviour primarily directed by the unconscious.

Decisions

If memories perpetuate beliefs, decisions are the cornerstones of beliefs. Something objective happens, then you make subjective decisions as to what to believe about life based on that objective event.

Life in the present reflects all the decisions you made in the past unconsciously.

Example: Two people can have the same experience and make very different choices based on that experience.

Two sales agents were told by their manager that they were useless and unable to reach the budget. One may decide that the manager is right, doubts himself and drops down, and the other may decide to prove the manager wrong and becomes the number one sales agent in the company.

Or your teacher told you that you are not good at learning and you believed it, until you decided to stop believing it, and proven her wrong by remaining a curious student enjoying growth.

Language

Analytical philosophers and linguists from Schopenhauer to Muller have asserted that it is language that allows people to take their minds to previously unexplored places and viewpoints. Language determines what people think about and how they see the world. The words you speak, hear, and see are translated in your mind and other people's mind as pictures. Since what we focus on is what we create, it is worth being aware of the words we use to express ourselves. Self-talk can be your worst enemy if fed with negative and bad words about yourself; replace them with kind and positive words.

Example: If you are looking to be wealthy, you need to increase your financial vocabulary, as it will expand your life view of what is monetarily possible. If you want to be successful in what you do, use success words, confident words, and motivating words.

Meta Programmes/Language and Behaviour Profile (LAB Profile) as an overview explanation

Meta Programmes are content free and have no information, they depend on a context and a situation lived. They are made up of a collection of thoughts and behavioural patterns. They include motivation direction, motivation source and reason, awareness of time, response to challenges, and direction of energy. Understanding Meta Programmes gives you more choices over how you choose to function. Recognising them in others helps in predicting people's actions, understanding and enhancing your communication with them. Some patterns elicitation I have covered and others I won't as they don't relate directly to the purpose of my book.

How do we trigger motivation and capture others' interests?

Motivation Traits

- Motivation Level (proactive, reactive).
- Motivation Direction (towards, away from).
- Motivation Source (internal, external).
- Motivation Reason (possibilities, necessities).
- Motivation Decision Factors (same experience, same experience with differences).
- Values (criteria).

How can you maintain someone's motivation?

Working Traits

- Information Chunk Size (specific, general).
- Working Attention Direction (self, others).

- Working Stress Response (feeling, thinking, or choice).
- Working Style (independent, cooperative, proximity, team player, manager).
- Working Organisation (person, thing).
- Convincer Mode (needs to see, hear, read or do to be convinced; with number of examples, or automatically convinced, or consistent proof, or convinced over a period of time).

Sources: NLP, Rodger Bailey's LAB profile and Shelle Rose Charvet *"Words that Change Minds"* book.

Cause > Effect Equation

Empowering Change

This equation led me to a lot of suffering. I stood most of my life at effect blaming everything and everyone for my unhappiness and emptiness. I can tell you, my whole life turned upside down when I clicked and finally decided to take responsibility for MY results. What a relief when I felt in control and excited about solving rather than blaming, walking rather than stopping, and smiling rather than crying.

To each cause, there is an effect. **A cause leads to a consequence.** You can always find excuses for why your results don't reflect what you want, and blame, accuse, or play the victim. The only way out for change is when you choose to be at cause, humbly analyse the situation, take ownership of it, and look for the solutions.

Cause	Effect
Results I am responsible for the results I produce	Reasons/Excuses I find excuses for not being in charge of the results I produce and find reasons to defend myself
HOW	**WHY**
Action	**No Action**
I am accountable	I am a victim Blame others and the environment
I am in control	I believe it's out of my control
Determined to succeed	Planning to fail
Looking for opportunities	Stuck in a situation
Effort	No effort
Change zone	**Comfort zone**
I choose to own my choices	I have no choice but I have secondary gains, such as support from the environment
Growth: learning from the situation in order to improve (mature) and grow	Blabbermouth, talker, gossiper, complainer, and giving up

**"EVERYTHING is my RESPONSIBILITY,
NOTHING is my fault.
Only FEEDBACK not failure."**

Source: CHC Fast Track To Success

"I am responsible for my results, in control of my destiny and not a victim of my story."

Larissa Redaelli

Cause > Effect Exercise

Think of a situation where you are currently at effect, finding excuses why you haven't achieved something the way you wanted or be the person you desired. A situation where you accuse or blame someone or something for the way you feel and make them responsible for your effect.

Write down

_____
_____
_____
_____
_____

You are at Effect.

How can you move to cause, putting yourself in an accountable role to find a solution?

Ask yourself:

1. How did I create it? Somewhere on the road of my existence, I wasn't born with this.
2. What do I want to create INSTEAD?

_____
_____
_____
_____
_____

You moved from effect to be at Cause.

"Let us not look back in anger or forward in fear but around in awareness."

James Thurber

Cognitive Behavioural Therapy

CBT is a form of psychotherapy that treats problems and boosts happiness by modifying dysfunctional emotions, behaviours, and thoughts. It is used to treat less severe forms of depression, anxiety, post-traumatic stress disorder, eating disorders, and borderline personality disorder. It is a first line of treatment for a majority of psychological disorders in children and adolescents, including aggression and conduct disorder. Unlike traditional Freudian psychoanalysis, which probes childhood wounds to get to the root causes of conflict, CBT focuses on the development of personal coping strategies that target solving current problems and changing destructive behavioural patterns consciously.

It is a **"problem-focused"** and **"action-oriented"** form of therapy assessing whether distorted thoughts (limiting beliefs) and feeling distressed are an accurate depiction of reality, and if they are not to employ strategies to challenge and overcome them, as when we are in pain, our perception of reality may be distorted.

By becoming aware of a few common thinking errors (distortions of reality) most of us can use self-help to break through them, bringing back happiness to life and healthy perceptions through thinking constructively, planning and taking action towards identifying and solving goals.

A think, plan, do, repeat pattern.

Usually a negative thought builds another negative thought that grows in bulk and drives you into a vicious circle in a racing thinking mode. They are called Automated Negative Thoughts (ANTs).

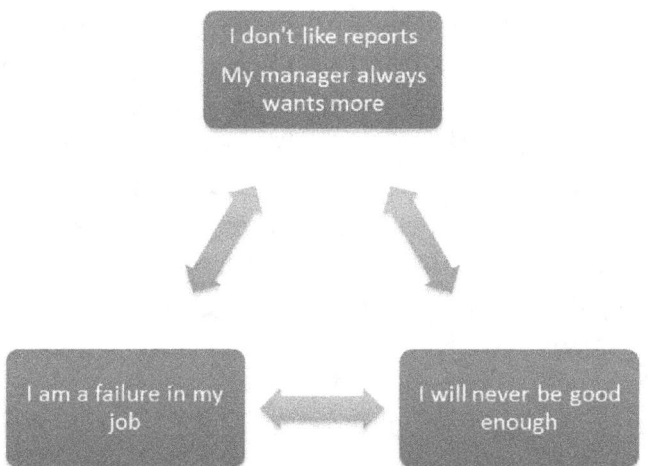

Before I explain which thinking errors I worked on, I will share with you one of the most painful thinking error that cost me a lot until I finally managed to get rid of it.

Expectations
The Beauty and the Beast

Expectations can be defined as your imagination of things likely to happen. What you want, wish, desire, need, and how you see it happen inside your mind. Good things or bad things. The reality is the actual state of events that happen from what was wished, needed, or wanted.

A tendency to make unrealistic and unreasonable demands on yourself or others. You put your sets of rules and wishes onto someone else and expect them to do it.

The question is, are the expectations met? The truth is, expectations are required for us to function and to be a part of society. For example, it is expected that you dress when you leave your house. If you didn't, people might be uncomfortable. Or your manager expects you to be on time and if you aren't, he wouldn't like it and might reprimand you. Or mothers expect their children to tidy up their room and study at school and if they don't, then they get angry with them. So, expectations have their place. But problems arise when we fail to give the right significance to these assumptions, such as expecting "more" or "less" from others and ourselves than we ought to. It is then that we set ourselves up for disappointment.

If you search on any website for information on expectations, you fall in the negative loop of the danger of expectations, most of all the negative advice on having them in the first place. It's true, nevertheless, if you just leave things to chance, you will get frustrated and then you are not in charge of your life. If you expect unrealistic things to happen, you are most likely not going to see them materialise and be greatly disappointed.

"My manager should know what I need," "I must get his attention," or "My mother should understand my situation."

Expectations need to be managed. And this is not the same as having none. Some people say, "Always expect the worst, and you'll never be disappointed." I would say, **"Express your expectations clearly, and you can anticipate miracles."** When I expect someone to behave in a certain matter and do not voice clearly my expectations to him or her, then I am frustrated with the result. Yet who is to blame? If you put yourself at cause, then you are responsible or, at least, you need to step back and analyse your part of the other person's behavioural feedback, moreover if you actively listened to their point of view and expectations, the result would have definitely been different.

How can you expect the other person to act exactly like you want them to, if they have no clue what you are predicting they would do? They are completely unaware as to what is going on in your mind. They have a different model of the world, different experiences, different values and beliefs, different personalities, different ways of functioning, different understanding, and different visions.

Expectations	Reality
Things to do (usually you say "must do")	Things you really do
Exercise	Next Sunday or Monday
Diet	Next week/overeat/eat unhealthy
Finish tasks	Procrastinate
Supermarket	Grumbling back home
Kids homework	Complaining/arguing with kids
Cooking	Forget a pinch of love

Another typical example in relationship is when you expect to be wrapped in your partner's arms when you tell him you are cold, and in reality, he replies back to you by saying, "You should have brought a jacket." Here you get so upset, disappointed, and frustrated. If you were clear on what you expected by voicing it out as "I would love to be in your arms, I am feeling cold," you would have got what you really expected.

I was like many other people, expecting so much from myself, from others, and from my environment. I was like this for half of my life until I started my awakening journey in search of answers for how I could be happy, fulfilled, grateful, and in control of my reality.

I started wondering if there could be another way to make expectations happen. What if I worded clearly what I expect, value, and believe, plan and take action accordingly? What if I was expecting the unrealisable? What if people around me were neither magicians nor mind readers? What if people around me did care? What if I could expect the best of myself and others, and actually got it? And how would I do that?

With the conscious awareness and the discovery of my true "I," my deepest "I," my real "I", and not my false "I" (my ego "I"), I learned how to create excellent results in my life, being in charge of my reality and in control of my thoughts, feelings, and behaviours. It's all about paying attention to what is going on inside your mind, what you are expecting, what is important to you, what you believe. Check your surroundings, ask, word, and understand by listening, leaving your pride aside.

Consider:

- Have you ever noticed that the results that you get are directly related to your expectation of what is going to happen?
- Have you ever heard that what you get is what you focus on?
- And could you change your thoughts? Your thoughts become your reality, so expect good things to happen. Be it great relationships, wealth, health, career or family success, fun, happiness, and anything else that you want.
- Create goals that are specific and write them down. Stick them wherever you can in order to have them always in your focus.

- Hold empowering beliefs about yourself and your ability to create the life that you want.
- And then take action!

What might be stopping you?

- A lack of clarity?
- A lack of goals?
- A lack of self-belief?
- A belief that you are not in charge of your life and that everything is against you?
- A negative emotional state?
- Are you idealising people, events, and the environment?
- A lack of communication or miscommunicating?
- Do you expect too much of yourself?
- Are there certain areas of your life where your expectations are high and others where they are low?

Ask yourself: **Do you want it badly enough? Are you worth it?**

"The key is to trust people to be who they are.
Instead, we trust people to be who we want them to be,
And when they aren't, we cry."

David Duchovny

"Blessed is he who expects nothing,
For he shall never be disappointed."

Alexander Pope

"I find my life is a lot easier the lower I keep my expectations."

Bill Watterson

"Everyone seems to have a clear idea of how other people should lead their lives, but none about his or her own."

Paulo Coelho

"We're wired to expect the world to be brighter and more meaningful and more obviously interesting than it actually is.
And when we realise that it isn't,
We start looking around for the real world."

Lev Grossman

"When you stop expecting people to be perfect,
You can like them for who they are."

Donald Miller

"You are your own worst enemy.
If you can learn to stop expecting impossible perfection,
In yourself and others,
You may find the happiness that has always eluded you."

Lisa Kleypas

"Make sure your worst enemy doesn't live between your two ears."

Laird Hamilton

"That was the thing about the world:
It wasn't that things were harder than
you thought they were going to be,
It was that they were hard in ways that you didn't expect."

Lev Grossman

"Set the standard! Stop expecting others to show you love, acceptance, commitment, and respect when you don't even show that to yourself."

Steve Maraboli

> "Happiness equals reality minus expectations."
>
> Tom Magliozzi
>
> **"Give expectations the right significance."**
>
> Larissa Redaelli

Below are some other thinking errors I worked hard on and the results are priceless, believe me.

1. **Catastrophising:** Magnifying positive attributes of another while minimising your own or blowing things out of proportion, making problems larger than life. "Today is the worst day of my life."
2. **Double standards:** If it's ok for you but it's not ok for someone else and vice versa. "If x doesn't get a raise it's fine, but if I don't, I will quit," or "It's ok if I do this, but if my husband did, it's not."
3. **Mind reading, feelings vs. facts and jumping to conclusions:** Imagining and assuming you know what someone else is thinking in the absence of evidence (sort of like fortune telling). "I know my superior is mad at me because he didn't talk to me this morning." Check for evidence. How do you know that what you think is true? Talk things over, ask for proof using open, genuine, and honest communication. What if there is another explanation for this?

4. **All or nothing thinking, or black and white thinking:** Looking at events in extremes with no in-betweens; the tendency to see things as all or nothing, good or bad, black or white, right or wrong. "There was nothing interesting at all in that meeting." Absolutely nothing?
5. **Labelling:** The tendency to make global statements about yourself or others based upon a situation. **Judging** and assigning labels to people based on their behaviour. "She's so arrogant," or "He lost his keys, he's so careless." Don't label the person; accept the person and change the behaviour. *Everyone* is doing the best they can with the resources they have available at that given moment consciously.
6. **Over-generalising:** The tendency to make broad generalisations based on a single event and minimal evidence. You conclude that whatever happened to you once will occur over and over again as part of a pattern, not as a one-off occurrence and it will happen in future relationships, future careers, or future opportunities. "I was late to deliver my report. I will never be good in administration," or "I missed going to the gym for two weeks. I will never find time to exercise," or "I ate a spoon of ice-cream during my diet. I have blown it completely."
7. **Personalisation:** Whatever people say or do is taken personally as a direct attack. Or blaming yourself or taking responsibility for something you didn't do. "It's my fault."
8. **Comparison:** When you compare yourself with others, what they have that you don't, what they are that you are not . . . Pure pain.
9. **Reward fallacy:** Expecting that whenever you do good, you need to be rewarded, and you feel frustrated when it doesn't happen. "I am working hard, this shouldn't happen to me." One habit I took is reward myself for

every achievement, even the smallest, to avoid any disappointment.
10. **Blaming:** Blaming others for something that was your fault, for how you feel, for your failures, for not achieving . . .
11. **Emotional reasoning:** The tendency to interpret your experience based on how you are feeling in the moment. Because we feel a certain way, we think it must be true. What evidence do you have that how you are seeing this is accurate?
12. **Mental filtering:** The tendency to focus on negative events while disqualifying and neglecting the positive ones.
13. **Forcing your partner and people to change, taking them for granted:** Display your care and accept the person.
14. **Using necessity words such as "should," "have to," "must":** Make you feel guilty, as if you already failed.

1. Recognise the Automated Negative Thought that takes place in your head.
2. Label it.
3. Stop and think by asking yourself: "Do I have evidence that supports this thought?"
4. Put the awareness light on and ask yourself: "What Constructive Automatic Thought can I replace this with?"

You need to replace your old thinking habit with a new one that benefits you. It takes time, patience, consistency, discipline, and, moreover, 100 per cent commitment to change.

"If you want to do something, you will find a way, if not, you'll find an excuse."

Jim Rohn

Replace ANTs by CATs Exercise

Think about a common situation when you experience distortion in your thinking (ANT) and identify a constructive thought to replace this thinking error.

Thinking errors	I experience this . . .	-Constructive thought -Beneficial reaction could be . . .
Unrealistic expectations		
Catastrophising		
Double standards		
Mind reading		
All or nothing thinking Black and white thinking		
Labelling/Judging		
Overgeneralisation		
Personalisation		
Comparison		
Reward fallacy		
Blaming		
Emotional reasoning		
Mental filtering		
Forcing partner and people to change		
Necessity words and guilt		

> "You will either find a way, or make one."
>
> Hannibal

> "You don't fix problems,
> You fix your thinking and then,
> Your problems fix themselves."
>
> Louise Hay

Faradarmani

A great year of descent to ascent and transcend.

Founded by Dr. Mohammad Ali Taheri, over forty years ago, it is an alternative medicine, completely mystical, and a subcategory of Inter-Universal *Erfan* (Divine Intelligence). The organisation, National Centre for Complementary and Alternative Medicine (NCCAM), has classified Complementary Alternative Medicine into five categories. Faradarmani falls under the fourth category of mind-body intervention. It's a qualitative treatment method without any kind of intervention in the quantitative process (classic conventional medicine) or any hardware manipulation. Man's existence is seen as vast as the universe itself, much more than just a composite of flesh and bones.

The universe is composed of matter, energy, and awareness. We are a collection of physical, psychological, mental, and other bodies with energy transformers (*chakras*), limited and blocked energy channels, various polarity, bioplasma fields, cellular consciousness, molecular frequency, and endless other unidentified parts. Since awareness is neither matter nor energy, it is not restricted to time or space, and treatment can occur over a short and/or long period.

Faradarmani is based on the theory of *Ettesal* (Grace), a consciousness bond where a link is established between the inter-universal consciousness and the consciousness of the mind in a matter of a flick of a finger, or *nazar*. Based on the nature of this *Ettesal*, some information is conveyed and the defective parts of the body are revealed in the form of seeing colours, light, movement, and energy throughout the body, with the feeling of heat, or pain, sharp aches or pulsation.

Through the scanning process, the inter-universal consciousness begins to investigate and scan the individual's countless constituents. Scanning includes the mind, psyche, and body, and is followed by a phase called "Externalisation," A process in which the symptoms of diseases and problems are revealed, and the person's history of illnesses is activated even back to the embryo or childhood stages. It may include current diseases, current undetected illnesses, hidden fears, emotional stress, and mental disorders. For a deep-rooted treatment to take place, one must allow the externalisation discharges and its manifestations to be completed with patience. Following externalisation, the signs and tensions disappear and recovery starts.

The objectives are:

- Understand the use of consciousness, **feel** the existential gratitude and divine intelligence.
- Understand inner values, recognise the inner treasures and knowledge of *Kamal* (transcendence beyond beauty and perfection).

- Achieve spiritual perfection and move from superficial life to a deeper one with connectedness with all beings to God in the world of love.
- Become free from the captive "Self."
- Service to people and practical worship.
- A way for public salvation.

Where does happiness come in? This practice goes beyond healing and beyond happiness, as it teaches you to become friends with your own being, as you poison it with illness, problems, and other negativity, because the veil that conceals your happiness is your own being. Happiness is found when you are one "as a whole," with all your being always connected to the Divine, THE source that can transform and free you from yourself, a positive change towards *Kamal* (spiritual completeness).

This school of thought assembled all my learning, allowing my biggest and most painful rise.

Through silence and a deep connection with the highest Energy Source **God**, I succeeded in tapping into the core of my onion and, I can tell you, it was a hard one. All the techniques I used cleaned a lot of my embedded and imprinted limitations, but there were lots I didn't tap into at the deepest level. By connecting and allowing the scanning to happen, they popped up for resolution.

I was sick, had pain all over my body, and I felt like I was in a tornado, trying to get out of the air column with speeds over what I could handle. But I was happy to welcome all this as I knew THIS IS IT, I am going to rise STRONGER THAN EVER, and I did.

I stopped all my medications, dealt with each externalised symptom revealed, and I freed myself from the most devastating and stacked memories, thoughts, and feelings that were forbidding me from being free and substracting me from experiencing sustainable happiness.

This is where I understood what inner calmness and silence meant. At the start, with my Faradarmani therapist, I thought I wasn't doing it right. But there is no right or wrong; it starts with the belief in God's healing, then the belief that you will, your commitment to allow whatever will be revealed, and dealing with the reply with all your faith, courage, and strength. No tools are used whatsoever. You can cure yourself through enlightenment (listen to your intuitions, welcome and understand the universe signals) to transcend, while eradicating pain and suffering.

The Power of Now by Eckhart Tolle

The secret behind finding our way out from psychological and body pain is to surrender to the present moment, the Now. Discover our true Being by embracing the silence, the space all around us, and all that exists right here, right now, to find deep inner peace.

Stop wasting time worrying about the future and regretting the past; each minute you spend on each of them is lost. Instead, live every minute in the present, now. Nothing exists outside the moment. All problems are illusions of the mind.

Eckhart Tolle found peace overnight, quite literally, after leading a very troubled problematic life punctuated by many periods of serious depression. Depressed by late-night thoughts, he started questioning what it was that made his life so unbearable where he couldn't stand himself any longer, and he found the answer in his "I." He wrote *The Power of Now*

(1997), a great enlightening manual that shook my life and helped me a lot during my self-therapy. There are so many lessons to learn. I will only highlight a few to help you worry and regret less:

1. Life is a series of present moments.
2. All pain is a result of resistance to the things you cannot change.
3. You can free yourself from pain by constantly observing your mind and not judging your thoughts.
4. Transcend from your ego "I" and discover the divine, complete, and perfect being that you are.
5. You are not your mind.
6. Connect with your true Being, the Higher Good, beyond Happiness.

My Application of the Power of Now

Eckhart Tolle made it clear to me that I was definitely on the wrong path and that I will only find freedom and happiness when I understand how much time I misuse and procrastinate thinking about yesterday and worrying about tomorrow. He lit my black tunnel in the hardest times, where I had only thoughts to divorce myself. These are the lessons I applied.

Lesson 1: All life is a series of present moments.

Ninety-nine out of hundred people would name their two most common bad feelings as regret and anxiety. The constant stream of consciousness thoughts played 24/7 in our heads, past and future thoughts. The past cannot survive in our presence, nor can the future. When you wake up ten minutes late in the morning, what's the first thing you think? "I overslept, I wish I hadn't hit the snooze button," closely followed by, "Oh no, now I'll be late for work, I'm sure my boss will be mad at me!" You have ruined at least the first half of your day.

Tolle says that the only important time that matters and the one we think about the least is **the present**. Everything we feel and sense takes place in the now. Living any other moment than the now is useless, as the past has gone by and the future is a collection of present moments waiting to arrive.

Example: If you have a project to hand in a month, regretting all the time you procrastinated or worrying about the big workload that is to come will not help you get there. But if you just start now with an outline, you can only move towards finalising the project.

Lesson 2: Any pain we feel results from resisting the things we can't change. We think a lot about the past and the future, but we can only live in the present, and we have no means to change the things we were unhappy about back then. So we fill the gap between these by developing resistance to them and experience psychological or physical pain. When we are angry, we think and act less rationally and experience worse situations thus, more pain.

Lesson 3: We can free ourselves from pain by constantly observing our mind and not judging our thoughts.

How can we get rid of the pain? Tolle recommends two things:

1. Constantly ask yourself: "What will my next thought be?"
2. Stop judging your thoughts and urges.

1. Asking yourself this question over and over will usually delay your actual next thought, giving you enough time to realise how

much you actually spend in autopilot mode. This way you can start interrupting your mind pattern and separating from it.

2. Listen to your body and learn to accept the constant nagging thoughts in your head about what you should or should not be doing. The next time if you wake up late for work, just listen to the voice that says, "You should have done better!" but don't act on it. Notice it, see it, accept that it's there, but don't give in to its advice. Don't let it control or obsess you.

These two tools will help you separate your body from your always on thought-driven mind, after which you'll be in less pain, because you will resist a lot less the things that you can't change. You will learn:

- How your ego stops you from being happy and what to do about it.
- What you can learn from Buddha's six-year abstinence about the wisdom of your body.
- How to live in the now by being in a state of permanent alertness.
- Why living in the present can be hard.
- What to do with the pain that isn't avoidable, like when a loved one dies.
- Why surrendering to the present does not mean you'll live a passive, boring life. Problems do not exist, they belong to the past. Fear and anxiety belong to the future.

I attended Eckhart Tolle's conference in Dubai on September 8, 2018, a gift of being, listening live to all his teachings. I will resume the notes I have taken.

A few affirmations of Eckhart were playing back to back on a screen with the song "Let it be," (The Beatles), while waiting for him to come on stage. They put me in a great awakening mood to what I was going to receive.

"Bring presence into whatever you do."

"You are not your mind."

"In you there is a dimension of consciousness far deeper than thought."

"Every time you create a gap in the stream of mind, the light of consciousness grows stronger."

"Accept this moment as it is."

"The source of all abundance is not outside you, it's part of who you are."

"Your life is NOW."

"Awaken to a life of purpose and presence."

"Whenever deeply you accept this moment as it is, no matter what form it takes, you are still, you are at peace."

"Your entire life consists of the present moment."

"Be compassionate with yourself."

Spiritual and Consciousness Awakening Talk
The Next Step To Human Evolution

His presence on stage gave me two hours of peace, inner calmness, and eagerness to listen. He started with explaining sufferance that arises since birth with the baby crying and the explanation of the term "awakening" used 2,500 years ago by Buddha. The awakening from a normal wakeful state to a higher deeper state of consciousness.

A gradual process from out of sleep to consciousness and normal consciousness to an awakened state of consciousness.

It begins when you first realise the voice in your head that comments, your inner monologue. Your identification with this inner voice is your thinking. You only know yourself as the thinker; that is what you believe. Your thoughts are conditioned by the past, every judgement, complaint, and critical voice. There is no separation with your thoughts nor voice. They are it. You are trapped in it. Reactive likes and dislikes. This identification makes life very unpleasant to you. There are days where you are drawn back to it.

How much useless complaining do you do a day? (Out loud or in your head.)

- Have said
- Have done
- Failed to say
- Failed to do
- Place where you are
- What you are doing
- Stuck . . .

This is a toxic state of consciousness where people carry this burden.

Who am I? The question that bangs in our head.

What is it that gives you your sense of self? Or identity?

"My life." You complain a lot about it. People carry this term "my life" and mix it with suffering and some hope of change someday. You pretend to be happy and imitate the Instagram and TV stars amplifying the human ego of happy, rich people, the "ok people."

Movement of thought + emotion

- Past
- Collective past from your environment
- Short past

= Me and my life. The human ego is conceptual, an ego since the creation of language.

Narcissist people carry their burden of the sense of self. What sticks in your mind? The good things or the bad things?

When you see beauty, it stops your thinking mind with an "oh." You are intensely present; you are not thinking. Accidently, you entered, for a few seconds, a state of conscious awakening "aaaaaaah"; there is no conceptualisation afterward; you just say that was a beautiful sunset. Your mind won't continue streaming on it. If someone did something bad to you, what happens? You enact an imaginary conflict situation, a blow of emotions, you build on it, what you should have said and didn't say, what you should have done and didn't do . . .

Conceptual reality, secondary reality . . . your mind loves dwelling on it.

The essential part of awakening is a gradual disidentification with this stream of thoughts, a not-dragged-along attitude, where you start to notice, to observe. There is a dimension in us where we can be aware and don't need to think. Our ability to think constructively will improve drastically. The mind that makes you unhappy decreases and the realisation that a greater part of the unhappiness experience in life derives from interpretation, a dysfunctional consciousness form of unhappiness.

The little things that make you upset cumulate until they create a huge unhappy self, looking for a cause.

- What is it that causes me to feel this?
- How would I experience this situation without the addition of the narrative?

Experience the situation as it is without asking "why me?." Be with the moment as it is; this is a shift; you are no longer in opposition with what is happening. You are ok for so little moments and for so many moments you experience huge amounts of unhappiness, of unconscious constant narrative thinking that inhabit you. It is easy to leave a place behind, but you can't leave your mind behind, your ego mind.

Allow "the isness of things" in your life and separate the "isness" from you. Be alert to moments in your life, free of thinking, with no labelling, no conceptual thinking, no opinion about yourself, and no judgment.

A dog has no conceptual sense of self; he doesn't care for his weight. He just is. The universal consciousness in the tree reflects how it is deeply rooted in being. You can learn how to be still from a tree, it just is.

The dog is halfway between the tree and you. He is happy 80-90 per cent of the time, his tail wagging, but the owner of the dog is unhappy 80-90 per cent of the time. The dog exists below thought. We humans, we are approaching the end, completely trapped in thought. Our sense of identity derives from thinking about ourselves, me, and my life. The dog doesn't have a mental image of himself; there is no self. Humans have a conceptual sense of thought of self, "I am _____." A personal sense of self, possessions, lack of possessions, a mental image of the body, knowledge, role, and job. Ego can't do much comparing with and then judging others. Those who have, I would judge as superficial. Example: If I am unhappy with my weight and look, I would judge a person whose body appearance is fitter than mine by saying: "They have nothing else to do while me, I am so busy and have no time to exercise."

Mentally created self-image creates your identity of self, which is ultimately alienated. You only experience suffering and unhappiness. You are continuously absorbed by thinking. One thought after another until you can't live with yourself any longer.

The Presence Formula could be resumed as:

- Me as the conscious.
- Separated from my thoughts.
- Me as the observer with no judgement.
- Disidentified from thoughts.
- Me vs. thoughts.
- Conscious presence vs. ego.

Disidentification Technique

Free yourself from compulsive thinking.

1. **Fall below thinking:** When you are tired and ready to sleep, halfway before sleeping, free yourself from your

problematic self without using any drugs or alcohol, they deflect your mind to treat suffering.
2. **Rise above thinking:** You are not your mind; your identity doesn't derive from your mind. Identity in terms of form (personal past, experience, and personality), gender (man or woman), physical form (body), or psychological form (culture/personality).

Is that all what you are?

You are much more than that. The dimension in you that is far deeper than conceptual identity can only be accessed when your mind is still. Where you don't remember your past and you don't have a future, so what is left?

An "I" that is more essential than your past or future, an "I" without reference to historical person; it's a deep "I," the essence of your identity; everything else is a fiction, a dream.

You are present, you are aware that you are aware, you sense perceptions in a state of awareness: visual, auditory, and kinesthetic, as an underlying consciousness aware of the thought. You are no longer trapped in your personality; you have it, but you are not trapped in it. You are beyond personality. You need it to express yourself and to pretend to be yourself.

We lose half of our life in doing, which is the obstacle to "I am." Awake and spend more time in being. Stop thinking and rise above thinking. Shut your mind off. The art of living is not to lose the deep sense of beingness; you need to find a balance between doing and being. Invite being into your life, practice when engaged in activities and non-activities. "Be" when you are waiting, wherever and whenever you are waiting.

Consciousness is divine; it emanates from the source, like light emanates from the sun. Stop creating dysfunction in your life and realise the essence of who you are: a divine consciousness.

Compassion, love, and empathy to others only come from your essence, not from your personality. You go beyond the human, you look at their beingness, beyond personality. You recognise the essence of yourself in the other. You recognise the other as yourself. For the world to change, there should be enough humans to go through the shift of consciousness, and it begins with you. The purpose of our life primarily is to embrace an arising new state of consciousness. What I do is secondary consciousness. Inner alignment with the present moment is key. Let go and be the presence to embrace deep happiness. Be life and do not walk around with the burden of life situations. Let go of the clutters in your mind and embrace stillness. Adopt a Zen mind, an alert mind, an empty mind from the weights of life situations and from your "ego." Have the courage to embrace a state of not knowing, perceiving without interpreting. There is a deep kind of knowing moment of wisdom, far deeper than intelligence. Intelligence without wisdom leads to madness of over-analysing. The great adventure to awakening to the Universe consciousness is your only way out.

Life is full of challenges, and through them, awakening happens. Through suffering, the way you deal with problems change, then you welcome them as a necessary part of this world's dimension. When you recognise that life is difficult, you accept it with no inner resistance, understanding that it's in the nature of life, and then, it's no longer strenuous. It's tough when you think, "This shouldn't be happening to me," or "Why is it happening to me?" or "I don't deserve this." ACCEPT COMPLETELY the isness of the moment in its form, what is, and let go by surrendering to the yes moment now and allow the Universal consciousness to fill the space around it.

Focus your full attention to what is happening now:

1. Be in contact with your surroundings, come to your senses by seeing, listening, touching, and, with it, step out of thinking.
2. The real essence is to become aware of yourself as the presence, be, I am, I see nature around me, I smell fresh grass… notice that you are fully alert.

I often listen to Eckhart Tolle's YouTube videos before I sleep. The next day, I repeat the video I liked, take notes of impactful messages, apply them, and observe the results.

Emotional Detox

Positive Psychology and Emotional Management

Positive Psychology is the study of our strengths, virtues, and the factors that contribute to a full and meaningful life.

I learned a lot from Dr. Martin Seligman founder of positive psychology (1998), who summarises it in five factors **"PERMA"**:

Positive emotions help us build our physical, intellectual, and social abilities to perform better at work and strengthen our relationships.

Engagement: When experiencing flow, concentration becomes laser-focused so that everything else seems to disappear, and the perception of time is altered. The incessant voice in our head quiets down and we lose self-consciousness. As a result, we increase our performance level and creativity. Mihaly Csikszentmihalyi, the author behind this theory, believes that happiness isn't something that simply happens. It is the product of us crafting our challenges that are neither too demanding nor too simple for our abilities.

Relationships: We have a need for connection and interactions with other people. It is important for us to share love with physical and emotional proximity. A great example of this is babies who depend on others and are unable to survive on their own. Psychiatrist Robert Waldinger's study has shown that people are happier based on the quality of their relationships.

Meaning (a continuous search or belonging to something bigger): We are meaning-making machines. Whatever we do, receive as information, or recall, has to have an interpretation, a label to be understood. As per Dr. Seligman, the level of well-being we experience can be affected by our choices, attitudes, and behaviours; there are no shortcuts. It takes effort, persistence, and significance to foster an enduring sense of well-being. We are constantly chasing pleasure, but if we fail to use our strengths towards something meaningful, belonging to something bigger, we won't experience a deeper sense of satisfaction.

Accomplishments (having realised tangible goals): Research and studies consistently show that if you feel personally involved in pursuing and achieving your goals, you are in better health than people who lack a sense of direction in their lives. Not all goals contribute equally to well-being.

Research shows that the goals that lead to well-being are personally meaningful.

Accomplishment is often pursued for its own sake, even if it doesn't increase positive emotions, meaning, or the quality of relationships.

I learned to commit to my goals, surrounding myself with positive caring people who are able to support me in my growth and removed negative toxic people who drain me with their negative influence (angry, jealous, unwilling, unaware, and uncoachable people).

"Happiness is an ongoing process of fresh challenges and it takes the right attitudes and activities to continue to be happy."

Ed Diener

Dialectical Behaviour Therapy

An effective therapy developed by Marsha Linehan (1993) that helped me manage overwhelming emotions and handle distress without losing control, nor act destructively. It guided me on how to stop and reduce the intense limiting feelings that were consuming me, in order to keep my balance.

Resilience five pillars:

- Self-awareness.
- Mindfulness.
- Self-care.
- Positive, strong connections.
- Purpose.

It taught me four important skills to replace unhelpful feelings:

1- *Distress tolerance* to better cope with painful events by building up resilience (a psychological strength to deal with stress, setbacks, crises, and life challenges) and giving ways to soften the effects of upsetting circumstances for a quicker recovery.

Resilience technique:

- Be aware and evaluate the difficulty (understand and state the obstacle).
- Listen to your inner feedback (body, mind, self-talk).
- Rectify your behaviour (regulate your emotions and extract strengths from your problems' driven thoughts).
- Create a new strategy, new action with new resources to overcome and focus on a growth mindset for empowering results.

2- *Mindfulness* helps you experience fully the present moment, nonjudgementally bringing your focus and complete attention to the present experience on a moment-to-moment basis and less on painful events from the past, or frightening possibilities in the future. It helps overcome negative judgements about yourself and others.

3- *Emotion regulation* helps you recognise and observe clearly each emotion without getting overwhelmed by it and without behaving in reactive ways. Emotions are taken as feedback and kept under conscious control.

4- *Interpersonal effectiveness* allows you to express your beliefs and needs by setting limits and boundaries while finding solutions to problems, and protecting your relationships with respect.

Few tips to strengthen your resilience

1. Embrace change.
2. Remain calm, in control, and consciously aware of the situation, with your full attention in the present moment.
3. Forgive and accept what is happening.
4. Don't dwell on negative thinking errors such as seeing crises as insurmountable problems.
5. Let go of the mental and emotional burden.
6. Think of solutions, not excuses.
7. Move towards your goals.
8. Build positive strong relationships and avert toxic relations.
9. Nurture and sustain a positive view of yourself.
10. Have a sense of humour.
11. Maintain a hopeful outlook by being optimistic and keeping things in perspective.
12. Enjoy nature; green is the colour that represents resilience, renewal, and optimism.
13. Take decisive actions and fully commit.
14. Find your purpose in life.

Life is full of challenges, and no matter how much falls on you, you will only bounce back when you accept, forgive, thank, and respond with a rising strategy.

"Champions are made in training. Keep practising, keep going, keep growing, and NEVER GIVE UP. **You are doing great."**

Larissa Redaelli

Emotions Wheel Exercise

Evaluate your emotional wheel by becoming aware of which feelings compose your regular experience. Choose a colour for the positive emotions and a different colour for the negative ones. Notice what emotions inhabit you more. Is there any action required to regulate your negative emotions?

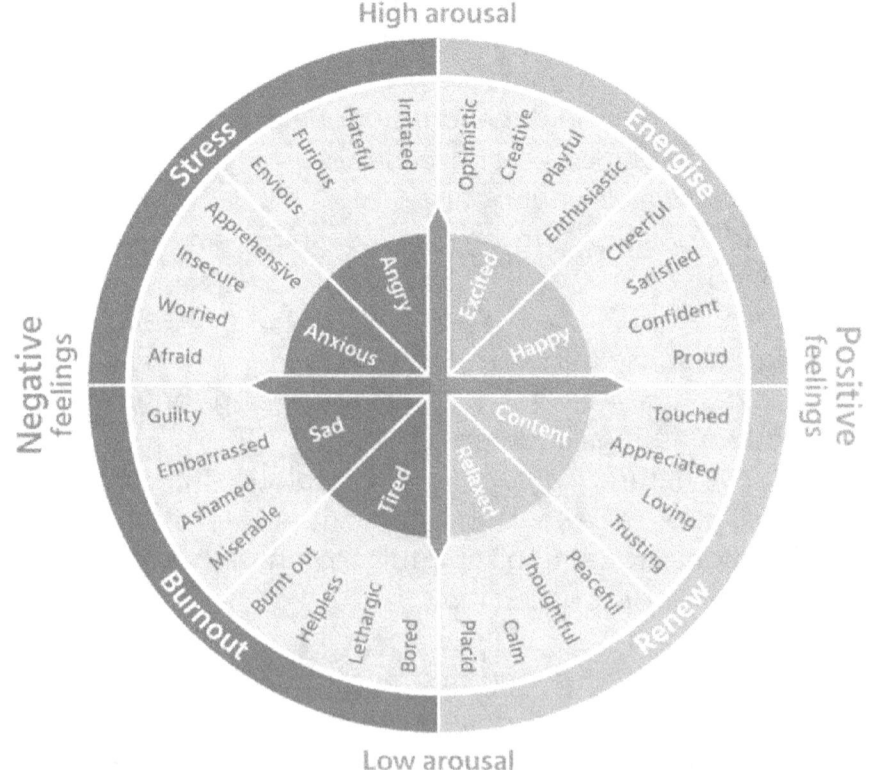

Source: jcaglobal.com

"Let the pain make you a Leader, Not a Monster."

Sunil Sindhwani

Emotional Intelligence

Emotions help you pay attention and assist you to cope with life complexities. The term "Emotional Intelligence" appeared for the first time in 1964. Then, after several papers were written on the subject. Psychologists Salovey and Mayer put forward an ability model in 1990 with regard to the capacity to reason about emotions, to enhance your thinking by accurately perceiving and accessing feelings, and to generate emotions that assist your thought in order to make decisions.

The Mayer–Salovey–Caruso Emotional Intelligence Test (MSCEIT) breaks emotional intelligence down into four competencies:

1. **Perceive emotions**: Recognise your own and others' emotions.
2. **Facilitate thought**: Generate and use emotions as problem-solving tools.
3. **Understand emotions** and how they can change.
4. **Manage your own and others' emotions**.

However, Daniel Goleman popularised it in 1995 in his book *EI, Why It Can Matter More Than IQ*, and defined it: "Emotional Intelligence is the ability to recognise your own feelings and those of others to motivate yourself and to manage emotions within and in your relationships."

He speaks about Personal and Social Competencies: Self-awareness of one's own emotions, self-management (regulation of negative emotions), and self-motivation. Social awareness of others' emotions includes empathy, compassion, and relationship management skills comprising: Conflict management, inspirational leadership, developing others, being a change catalyst, building bonds, encouraging teamwork, and collaboration.

It is about:
- Balancing emotions with logic and reason.
- Using emotions to enhance your thinking and solve problems.

Emotions can be an obstacle:

- If you feel that you lack objectives.
- If you feel anxious.
- If you are afraid of what others might think, or you fear to fail, fear to make mistakes.
- If you have poor self-esteem and low self-confidence.

Emotional Intelligence Model

I- Self-Awareness: Know your emotions.

Recognise and understand your emotions:

- How am I feeling? Sad, angry, doubtful, hurt, guilty, scared, anxious, overwhelmed, disempowered, stressed-out . . .
- What actually happened?
- Who said or/and did what? When?
- What results am I producing?
- What thought, emotion, behaviour, and action can empower me to overcome?

Assess your strengths, weaknesses, and limits. Be confident and fully accept that you are vulnerable to certain negative feelings. These can be overcome when you become conscious of the results they produce.

II- Self-Management (Emotional Regulation):

- Self-control: Control your emotions so they don't control and obsess you. Remain composed and focused under pressure.

- Self-regulation: Balance between expressing your feelings and avoiding unnecessary tension, by differentiating between good pressure and bad pressure, and no pressure.
- Use emotions as a problem-solving tool to facilitate your thoughts to effectively guide your decisions.

Tools to Regulate Your Emotions and Gain Self-Control

My Quick-Fix List

1- **Control your anger:** The strongest negative emotion we feel is anger, as through anger, many underlying negative emotions are triggered.

Anger Regulation Process

Use mnemonic words "AH FOWL" to remember the components of the Angela De Angelis process:

A	**Anger**	What made me angry, upset, fed up? Who said or/and did what?
H	**Hurt**	Sadness, pain, disappointment, What harm it did/does to me?
F	**Fear**	Afraid of what? Of who? Is it about me? And/or about others? What will happen next? What if the worst scenario occurs?
O	**Own Part**	Regret, accountability. How did I allow or trigger this situation? What is my part of responsibility?
W	**Want**	What do I want or wanted to happen? What do I deserve or need (ed)?
L	**Love**	What I appreciate, am thankful for? What did I learn? Who did I forgive?

2- Use **dissociation techniques** to detach from the negative emotions.

- Observe (witness) yourself, as if a second person is looking at you, as if you are watching a movie. You are the spectator looking at the actor (you). Use **reason vs. emotion, thinking vs. feeling**.

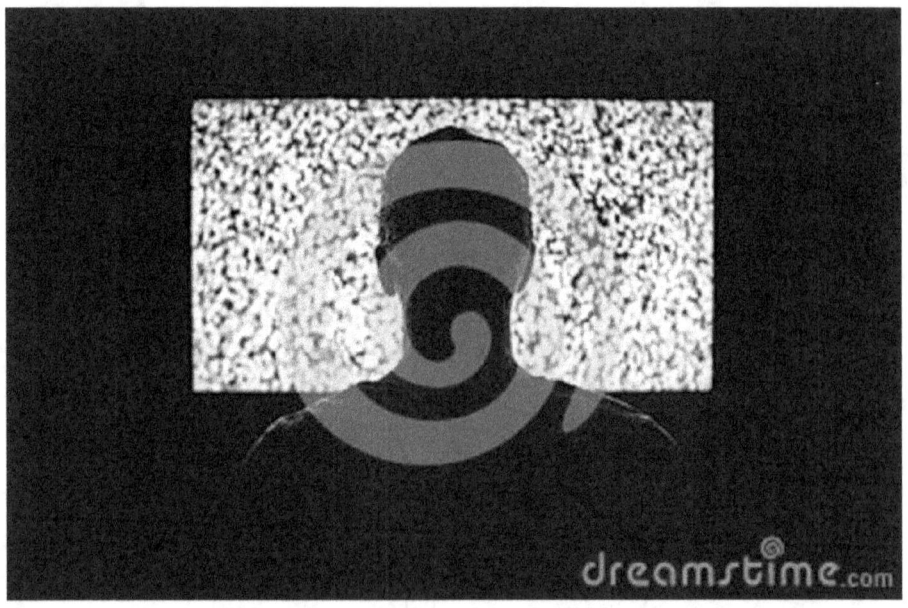

- Or adopt the **plane technique**, where you rise above earth in your mind, imagining you are in a plane, and you are looking down on earth, which represents your problem. Use your conscious awareness with the observer's eyes to look at how you can solve the problem, by thinking solutions rather than feeling the problem's pains. You are completely detached from it, as if you are in a bubble, and the problem stays out of it.

Or write, think, solve: Remove yourself from the negative thought by defining the problem and writing it down; it gives you a greater chance to deal with it logically and rationally, from a different perspective allowing you to think of a constructive thought that can replace the bad feeling of being trapped. You will see and attract solutions.

3- **Fix your posture**: Sometimes just by changing our body language, we can change the way we feel and think. Straighten your back in a superhero pose; open your chest, lift your face up, smile, "Fake it until you make it," this will bring your mind and body back into balance.

4- **Distract yourself**: Go for a walk to breathe some fresh air, go shopping, exercise, walk in nature, get a massage . . . **Change the environment** . . .

5- **Set clear, concise, realistic, and measurable objectives**: **Get started** and **commit yourself 100 per cent.** Think and focus on what you want. Write it down.

6- **BELIEVE in yourself**, believe you CAN. Acknowledge your strengths and focus your attention and energy on them. They are YOUR ASSETS.

7- **Work on your weak points**: They are your potential strengths.

8- Adopt the **champion's mindset**. Welcome, thank, and encourage inner feedback for rectification and constructive opinion from others. We have a lot to learn, even from people we least expect to acquire knowledge from. Champions are made winners by setbacks.

"Winners train, losers complain."

Red Auerbach

9- **Manage conflicts consciously**: They are a means of discovering yourself and others, while building stronger relationships. What are you projecting on others that you need to correct in yourself?

10- **Focus your lenses on the pluses of situations:** Analyse the minuses and gain understanding from them.

Life is CHANGE (seasons change, people change, day changes to night, emotions and thoughts come and go). Look at the possibilities and value change.

11- **Be at cause** by asking yourself: What can I do **NOW** to move forward? **HOW** can I find a solution to this? Instead of being stuck in, "Why does it happen to me?" you are in charge of the results you produce.

12- Remember, the choice is yours to be happy or to be sad, to be a success or a failure.

EXPECT success, you GET success.

Larissa Redaelli

13- **Reward yourself** upon any achievement; treat yourself, you deserve it! Remember, "What you appreciate, appreciates." Lynne Twist.

14- **Invest time and money in** personal development to sponge out what you soaked in during your imprint period, and create new neuro-pathways for change in your thinking to better your future. Unlearn and reeducate your mind with new constructive habits that will take you where you want to go. The best dividend for Return On Investment is YOU.

15- **Change your focus** and be attentive to the meaning you give to your experience. Remember, Frankl's saying, "Men are in search of meaning," and Alfred Korzybski's, "There's no inherent meaning to anything." Meaning is context and process dependent. We interpret our experience and then live with it. **Change your story narrative** if it's not working for you.

16- **Be resourceful**: It's not a question of resources, it is a question of resourcefulness. Remember that you have all the resources you need to succeed at the unconscious level! Be better than you were yesterday.

17- Download **mindfulness** applications to use for relaxation: meditation, deep breathing, visualisation...

18- Pray to energise.

19- **Use coping thoughts**: "All will be fine," or "Every day, I am getting better and better." Or, "I can do this," "I have faith and courage to face anything." "Everyday, I am a better version of myself."

20- Make a **happy list of meaningful songs, empowering proverbs** and **positive affirmations** with pictures and make them accessible at any time **to lift you up**.

"WHATEVER YOU DO, DON'T WOBBLE."

Socrates

21- My Signature **"4 × 4" Positive Thinking Formula:**

> **Think positive:**
> **4** minutes when you wake up,
> **4** minutes on the way to work,
> **4** minutes on the way back home,
> **4** minutes before you sleep.

Keep repeating this mantra loud with a BIG smile:

**I have Faith,
I am Healthy,
I am Happy.**

22- **Be present**, bring your attention in the **NOW:** Appreciate and enjoy what you can feel, hear, smell, taste, breathe, touch, NOW. When you are in the present moment, there is no past and no future. It's only here and now that you can decide, do, be, and have. It's in the now that you can change and create a better tomorrow.

"Don't wait for the perfect moment,
Take the moment and make it perfect."

Zoey Saward

23- **Be Grateful**: What are you grateful for having in your life? Write it down.

THANK YOU for . . .

_____
_____
_____
_____

Make this a morning ritual. Every day when you wake up, list three things you are grateful for, regardless of how you feel when you wake up. Install a Gratitude Habit; it improves your mental strength and emotional intelligence. It increases your happiness level, your self-esteem, and it attracts more things and people to be grateful for (the law of attraction).

You focus less on worries and allow more headspace to access mental resources to be productive in your day-to-day life.

"Gratitude turns what we have into enough."

Melodie Beattie

"Expect nothing and appreciate everything."

Louise Armstrong

24- **Love yourself:** Stay healthy and physically fit.

Make a daily routine schedule to be highly productive:

- Wake up between 5:30 a.m. and 7:30 a.m.
- Exercise for an hour to awaken your muscles after hours of no movement: Brisk walk for thirty minutes, or walk for an hour, or jog for twenty minutes and stretch.
- Meditate for fifteen minutes and visualise your meaningful goals.
- Pray.
- Be grateful for three things.
- Forgive yourself and others.
- Drink plenty of liquids (minimum two litres of water and herbal teas).

- Eat five healthy meals at the same timings: Have breakfast, morning fruit, lunch, afternoon healthy snack and dinner.
- Take half an hour to an hour to do something else you love: reading, massage, relax…
- Spend quality time with your loved ones.
- Stop all screens an hour before going to bed.
- Drink a bedtime sleep and relax infusion, caffeine-free, such as Chamomile, Valerian root, Lavender, Passionflower, Lemon balm . . .
- Take deep breaths for ten minutes and sleep before 10:30 p.m. (for seven consecutive hours minimum).

25- My Fulfilment 3Ps Formula:

Proud
People
Perform

Self-Leadership Guaranteed Empowering Values for Success

- Courage.
- Believe in yourself.
- Humility: Use pride when appropriate.
- Responsibility for learning and growth is yours.
- Flexibility to adapt to changing situations and overcoming obstacles.
- Commitment: 100 per cent determination and persistence.
- Discipline to be and do whatever is necessary to be happy.
- Positive: Seeing the upsides in everything.

> "If my mind can conceive it,
> And my heart can believe it,
> Then, I can achieve it."
>
> Muhammad Ali

III- Self-Motivation:

- Work towards a purpose and be driven by gaining pleasure. Hold the vision and trust the process.

> "The secret of getting ahead is getting started."
>
> Mark Twain

- Don't compare yourself to others.
- Make a conscious effort to not give up; keep trying, keep doing and keep the momentum. **When you feel like stopping, think about why you started.**
- Believe you CAN and act as if it is impossible to fail.
- Follow what is important to you, what you value most.

> "Do one thing every day that scares you."
>
> Eleanor Roosevelt

"The best view comes after the hardest climb."

Mahatma Gandhi

IV- Social Awareness:

- Empathy: Sensing others' emotions, putting yourself in other people's shoes. Understanding their perspective. Care from the heart, and take an active interest in their concerns. Your experience isn't their experience.

V- Relationship Competencies to Develop Strong Bonds:

- Positive influence and compassion persuasion with a win-win spirit.
- Caring and developing others.
- Change catalyst.
- Teamwork and collaboration.
- Create bonds that last, built on trust, and open genuine communication.
- Manage conflicts rationally.
- Lead by example and walk your talk.

At least 70 per cent of us do not live in the moment; we function on autopilot, not connected to our core purpose, reacting to our emotions, and not acting in line with our values and beliefs. We get lost in "ego."

We have been granted mental capacities to develop ambitious plans, beautiful bodies to act, and precious hearts to make connections, yet we make no time to live. We turn around complaining about not having authentic leaders, inspiring connections, engaging workplaces and environments.

If you can't find an authentic leader driven by purpose, be one.
If you can't find an inspiring connection, initiate one.
If you can't find an environment to thrive in, create one.
Build a bridge between your brain and your heart; they have the BEST of creations for us.

Emotional intelligence assisted me in monitoring my own and other people's emotions, by understanding and recognising them. I learned to label them appropriately and use the emotional information to enhance my thinking, my behaviour, and my decision-making.

I also enriched drastically my social relatedness, adding more empathy and cherishing the meaningful relations that sometimes I took for granted. As well as decluttering limiting relationships.

The Secret by Rhonda Byrne

> "As above, so below.
> As within, so without."
>
> The Emerald Tablet (3000 BC)

I read this book about ten years ago and it spread my awareness and made me think about all my perception errors. I definitely recommend it to beginners in their search for understanding life. It distils the teachings of centuries-old secrets by the most prominent people in history, great thinkers, and modern-day teachers. The awareness of the secret will bring inner light to overcome challenges and achieve what we may regard as impossible.

I gathered many important learnings from this book and I keep applying them.

"Like attracts like," says Richard Bach, because you are the law of attraction, the most powerful law in the universe, and the greatest secret of life.

Thoughts are magnetic and are sent out in the universe with a frequency that will magnetically attract like things on the same frequency. Everything sent will come back to you. Your current thoughts create your future.

> "What you resist, persists."
>
> Carl Jung

What you perceive or hold in your mind in terms of thoughts about yourself or others, attract the same thoughts, people, actions, and results. The more sustained the thought is, the more you give your attention and focus to it, and the law of attraction moves into action and delivers more thoughts of it, whether positively or negatively.

We become our thoughts.

This law was first recorded in a stone around 3000 BC; ancient Babylonians knew of it. Thoughts and images held in your mind act like a force that attracts and forms your entire life experience.

- If you think poor, you attract poverty;
- If you think abundance you allow abundance.

But if you then think fearfully of losing the wealth, thoughts of loss and fear become your dominant thoughts, and you will end up losing it. The law responds to your thoughts no matter what they are.

Bob Proctor summed up in three words, "Thoughts become things." You might as well direct them in the right direction of happiness. We are the most powerful transmission tower in the universe. Our transmission creates our life and the world through the frequency we use when thinking.

- See yourself how you want to be, and you will attract it.
- Attract what you want, rather than what you don't want.
- Think and speak about what you want, rather than what you don't want. By thinking, "I don't want him to disrespect me," I am attracting and wanting disrespect not only from him. The same goes for, "I don't want to argue," I attract more arguing.

Make your last thoughts before sleeping good thoughts. What you are thinking now creates your future life. If you are complaining, the law of attraction will powerfully bring into your life more situations to complain about; if you listen to someone complaining and you agree with them, you attract situations to complain about. Change the way you think; choose your thoughts consciously and remember that there is no such thing as a hopeless situation.

Affirmative thoughts are more powerful than negative thoughts, so when the negative manifests, change the thinking. Be the master of your thoughts, decide what you want to be, do, and have, emit the frequency, and your vision becomes reality.

Emotions tell you what you are thinking about and on what frequency you are on. The highest frequency you can emit is the feeling of love.

Feelings are an immediate signal of our thoughts. If they are bad feelings, such as anger, guilt, and fear, they result from bad thoughts, where you are in effect requesting for more of those. Think what joy, love, gratitude, and feelings of fulfilment can do for you, and how your thoughts can draw more things to make you feel good.

> Ask yourself: "What am I thinking about?
> What am I attracting right now? How do I feel?"

The more you think positive, the more you emit a powerful frequency that attracts good things and makes you feel good. Feelings are our best feedback to tell us if we are on or off-track. Don't allow negativity to change your mood. Use your feelings purposefully to transmit more power to what you want and desire. Feel the love that is surrounding you even if it is not. The universe will respond. Lift yourself with good intentions.

If you feel down, do something about it immediately; think of something beautiful, remember empowering memories, listen to a song you love, hug someone you care about, say affirmative positive words, and that will change your emotions and your thoughts. Create your **"Secret Shifters list"** and focus on one of them. Believe that the universe is supporting you in everything you do. Think of life as good and easy rather than hard and a struggle. You deserve all the good things life has to offer. Your wish is the universe's command. Figure out what will help if you generate the feelings of having it now. Do whatever you have to do to generate the feelings of having it now. You may wake up and it's there or you might get an inspired idea of some action to take, to be in the flow of the universe and to be open to welcome opportunities.

The Secret's Creative Process (taken from the Bible New Testament):

1. **Ask.**
2. **Believe.**
3. **Receive.**
4. **Be grateful.**

Apply the creative process, "How it will happen," is not your part. Trust the universe.

Step 1: **Ask**

"Ask in prayer, believe and you shall receive."

Bible, Matthew 21:22.

Make a command to the universe; let it know what you want. It will respond to your thoughts. Write clearly what you want in the present tense. What exactly do you want?

Complete the sentence: "I am happy and grateful now that. . . ."

_____

Step 2: **Believe**

Place your order once, as if you have ordered on the internet. Don't doubt if it has been received as you normally won't be placing the order several times. Believe it is already yours the moment you asked.

"Believe the unseen," said Lisa Nichols.

Have complete faith and get on with your life. The things you asked for will come to you; let them come. Don't worry about them or about your lack of them. Think of them as yours. If your thoughts are filled with not having yet, you will continue to attract not having it yet.

Act, speak, and think as though you are receiving it now. The universe is a mirror of your dominant thoughts. Emit the feeling frequency of having received it. The law of attraction will move all circumstances, people, and events for you to receive.

> "Let your faith be bigger than your fear."
>
> Bible, Hebrews 13:6

If you try to work out how it will happen, you are emitting a frequency that contains doubt. You think you have to do it and don't believe the universe will do it for you. The how is not your part of the creative process.

"You don't know how it will be shown to you, you will attract the way," said Bob Proctor. Frustration, disappointment, and doubt will shift your thoughts and attract the nonhappening. Replace these feelings with unconditional faith, and trust it's on its way.

Step 3: **Receive**

Feel wonderful about it now, the way you will feel once it arrives. Be on the good receiving frequency.

Write down and say to yourself:
"I am receiving now (fill in your desire) ---------------------------."

Trust your instinct; it is the universe communicating with you on the receiving frequency. Be a magnet with a clear mind of what you want, have faith, believe, and know it is coming your way. Remember, humankind began with one thought and manifested from the invisible into the visible. Time is just an illusion.

Praise and bless everything in the world, and you will dissolve negativity and discord. Align yourself with the highest frequency in the universe: God's love. Everything is energy. You are an energy pull. We are creators not only of our own destiny, but also of the universe. There is an unlimited supply of ideas, energy, knowledge and discoveries available in the universal mind. Drag it towards you, stay aware, and remember to remember, the power is in your thoughts.

The ten Secret Insights that helped me transform

1- My reaction to what happens in life dictates what happens next. The combination of thought, belief, and feeling in action responds to situations.

2- Negative thoughts are not true. My belief in negative thoughts makes them appear to be true, but it is not the reality.

3- Letting go allows for manifestation. I let go of my resistance for what I don't have yet, as I create the absence of what I want. I am ok with not getting what I want. It will manifest.

4- My suffering and struggle come from believing the untrue. Negative stories are a fabrication of my mind; suffering will be the consequence and physical pain. I stop telling and believing negative stories.

5- I am not in conflict with anyone or anything. Conflict attracts more conflict. Fighting against something, attracts more things to fight against.

6- Nothing stays the same; tomorrow, things will be different. Energy constantly changes. I stop giving attention to what is disturbing me; tomorrow, things will be different.

> "Where Attention goes, Energy flows.
> Where Intention goes, Energy flows."
>
> James Redfield

7- I don't resist negative emotions, as resistance will hold them. They are energy and will pass by quickly.

8- I judge least, I have few opinions and conclusions, and I will feel joy.

9- Allowance eliminates suffering.

10- I am aware and I am here NOW. I don't listen to the narration in my mind. When I am driving, I am in the car and not lost in my thoughts. When someone is talking to me, I listen, I focus on what they are saying, and not on the talking in my head. Be alive with no thoughts, no problems, and no suffering; only joy of presence, here and now.

Environmental Detox

It is very important to analyse how the environment impacts you. In my case, I had to take the decision to leave my country, city, home, and have a deep cleanup of people who were toxifying me, and I did this several times. The first big move was leaving Beirut, my roots, my family, my friends, my "home," to a completely unknown place at the age of eighteen with nothing except a Swiss passport and poor luggage.

At several occasions, I left work environments which were putting me down and where I wasn't aligned with my managers' values, even though I shared the same company values, but I didn't agree nor comply with some of the leaders' misuse of power. There is no right or wrong. It is a question of willing to accept what you are surrounded with, be it colleagues, leadership style at work, customers, environment, family, friends or relations. If you evaluate the whole situation and accept to keep on going, then you have taken the decision, and you need to change the way you think about it; moreover how it affects you, in order to pursue and be able to perform.

What is important is that you become aware that your surroundings can cause you to be unhappy. Your awareness, analysis, and decision-making are key to your mental and physical health.

I have moved thirty-five times in my life to fourteen different countries and in each destination whenever I felt oppressed by my job, my environment, my managers, and at times customers, or relations, I would step back, bring calm and clarity in order to make the right decision in that particular moment.

I learned to detach myself from material possessions. I mean, stop stocking stuff at home or in my closets. I went through over fifty cleanups out of which two were the hardest emotionally. I sorted what I couldn't live without, what was necessary, happy things I wanted to keep and got rid of so many things related to sad memories, unnecessary objects, furniture, clothes, shoes, bags, belts . . . that were not only being piled up but could serve and make someone else happy. I never felt lighter. Now I move houses so easily and feel content.

In terms of my relations, I learned to categorise relationships:

- **My Nest**: My adorable husband and children to whom I am FULLY dedicated with all my being.

- **Family**: Healthy connections that truly love me, care for me, and participate in my growth. Those who are happy for my achievements. It goes without saying that I share a deep connection with them too, and would do anything for them.

  Some of my family members unintentionally manipulate and block me, or put me down, and stop me from moving with their advice monologues based on their own experience, or thoughts. I just ask them to not interfere in my development, thanking them for their care, yet transmitting the importance of them respecting my space and decision.

  Unhealthy family members: Those that intentionally are mean to me or jealous, and for whatever reason their presence around me is toxic, with all the pain this causes. I separated from them after having tried by all means to preserve the relationship. I couldn't force them to make things work if they didn't want to. I just forgave them and let them go.

- **Friends**: There's a saying "We don't choose our family, we get to choose our friends."

  Best friends: Those who are there for the good and the bad times, like in marriage. With whom I share everything, and where I am truly me in the relationship. No masks, no gloves, just being myself.

  One-way friends: The ones that are there for you when they need something. I kept those that I enjoyed being with, and removed the toxic ones after realising how much negative impact they had on me, and that their presence in my life was only beneficial to them, not to mention how damaging they were to me.

- **Social fun connections:** where you don't speak about your private stuff, but you enjoy hanging around with and just have fun.

- **Necessary connections**: required for my personal and professional development.

- **Work and business relations**: Ex-colleagues, managers, customers, suppliers... The same applied in my work relations. Cherish the people who lift me up, the positive connections, the mutual winning spirit and those who are willing to participate in my growth.

  I removed toxic connections dispatching envy, anger, power, meanness, unkindness, disrespect... Nevertheless, I do consider if their behaviour was intentional or unintentional before I take any decision or action.

I am a fully dedicated person and I value authenticity, empathy and care. I hate conflict, injustice, manipulation, and dishonesty in all its forms. I can't sleep if I have any misunderstanding or conflict with any person; I do whatever it takes to clarify and sort things out, even if I am not at fault. I put myself at cause and give it a try. But if the other person wants to stick to victimisation, pride, and ignorance, I learned to stop worrying about the relation, and let them go.

I went through a lot of pain and growth in my relationships, and I finally understood that we need to say no when yes isn't the answer, when things don't feel ok, nor make us think right. I now value fixing relationship boundaries to avoid any toxification.

There is nothing like mutually healthy relationships where both parties enjoy open communication with care, respect, kindness, and empathy; where you don't need to continuously prove yourself, battle, and wear masks to be accepted.

Question to you

Can a continuous search for happiness create unhappiness?

Think about it; seeking all the time, breathless, non-stop . . . for happiness can cause unhappiness, as you are no longer living, nor being. You are thinking and questioning all the time, whether or not you are happy in this moment, in this situation, in this discussion, in this role . . .

Relax.

Intensely enjoy each second, no matter who you are, where you are and what you do in life.

Just be, be happy with what is and always grateful.

Nutrition

"We are what we eat." Food affects our mind; it increases or decreases energy production, besides the brain and organs' functions. It oxidises (increasing toxicity levels and adverse effects) or benefits our body. There are so many books, studies, and articles on how and what to eat.

All my life, I struggled with weight, yo-yo energy, and diets. I would summarise my experience by saying: Eat five times a day, small portions, as organic and natural as possible. The best diet that helped me maintain my weight is a healthy Mediterranean diet. The main meals are composed of one-fourth protein, one-fourth carbohydrate (pasta, rice, bread, etc.), and half vegetables. It comprises a good breakfast to start the day, two healthy snacks (mid-morning and mid-afternoon), and eating the last meal by 7:00 p.m. Avoid sugar and carbs after 5:00 p.m. Food is assimilated and digested more efficiently during daytime than night time.

Your main course plate combination

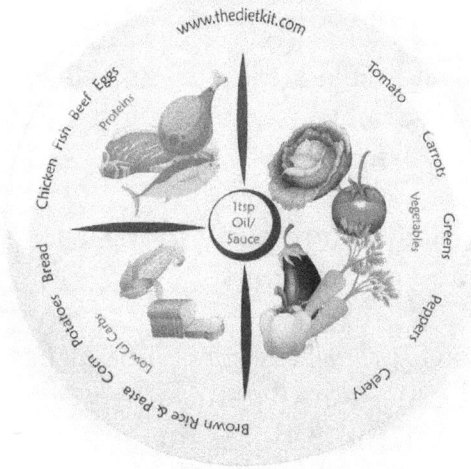

Source: thedietkit.com

Your diet should include essential vitamins, minerals, oils, and antioxidants. Avoid antinutrient overload and empty calories (the intake of C.R.A.P. foods).

The intake of empty calories consists of fat, processed foods, snacks, refined sugar, and refined flour. The calories in sugar are called empty as they provide no nutrients.

C.R.A.P. foods are not only empty calories but also contain ingredients that rob your body of essential nutrients, making you feel tired, and are dangerous to your health when overconsumed. They trigger overeating and cause you to put on weight.

Carbonated drinks: One of the main causes of today's obesity epidemic is due to overconsumption of soft drinks (coke, lemonade, milkshakes, natural or concentrated fruit juices).

Refined sugar: white flour, refined sugar, and high fructose corn syrup. Combined with pastries, cakes, cookies, yoghurt, and cereals.

Artificial colours, chemical additives, and flavourings: included in confectionery products (sweets, candy), soft drinks, party foods, snacks, and crisps.

Processed foods: ice-cream, party foods, sausages, hams, deli meats, smoked, and cured meats.

A variety of natural foods will help provide all essential nutrients, including helpful promoters (vitamins) to maximise the positive effects of each nutrient, reduce, minimise, or eliminate your exposure to adversaries (heat, light, alcohol, coffee, smoking, alkaline agents, overcooking, food refining/processing, antibiotics, and environment). Vitamin deficiency symptoms are wide, from lack of energy, insomnia, headache, poor memory, irritability, tension, muscle cramps, exhaustion, stress, skin symptoms, and indigestion to depression.

Example: **Vitamin C** (ascorbic acid) is effective to strengthen your immune system and fight infections. It produces collagen, keeping the bones, skin, and joints firm and strong. It is an antioxidant, detoxifying pollutant, and protects against cancer and heart disease. It helps make anti-stress hormones and turns food into energy.

Deficiency symptoms: frequent colds, lack of energy, frequent infections, easy bruising, slow wound healing, and red pimples.

Top foods: peppers, cabbage, broccoli, kiwi, orange, grapefruit, lime, tomato.

Promoters: Bioflavonoids in fruit and vegetables increase its effect. Works with vitamin B to produce energy and with vitamin E as an antioxidant.

Adversaries: smoking, alcohol, pollution, stress, and fried foods.

A-Z Essential Nutrients

The essential nutrients present in TOP foods should be in your shopping list.

Vitamins and their benefits

Nutrients	Benefits	Food sources
Vitamin A (Retinol and Beta-Carotene)	Healthy skin. Anti-inflammatory and immune system booster. Essential for night vision	Beef liver, carrot, sweet potato, tomato, broccoli, apricot, papaya, melon, cabbage, pumpkin, mango
Vitamin B1 (Thiamine)	Energy producer, helps brain functioning, and the use of protein in the body	Watercress, lamb, asparagus, zucchini, mushrooms, peas, lettuce, beans, tomato, Brussels sprout, cauliflower
Vitamin B2 (Riboflavin)	Turns fat, sugar, and protein into energy. Repairs and maintains a healthy skin. Regulates body acidity. Important for hair, nails, and eyes	Mushrooms, cabbage, bamboo shoot, wheat germ, milk, mackerel fish, asparagus, broccoli
Vitamin B3 (Niacin)	Energy producer. Helps brain and skin function. Balances blood sugar and reduces cholesterol levels. Aids digestion and is an anti-inflammatory	Mushrooms, tuna, chicken, salmon, cabbage, lamb, turkey, tomato, whole wheat, cauliflower
Vitamin B5 (Pantothenic acid)	Energy producer. Controls fat. Essential for brain and nerves. Healthy skin and hair	Mushrooms, watercress, broccoli, lentils, peas, strawberries, eggs, avocado, whole wheat, celery
Vitamin B6 (Pyridoxine)	Essential for protein digestion and hormone production. Balances sex hormones. Antidepressant, and diuretic. Helpful in menopause	Cauliflower, banana, squash, broccoli, red kidney beans, seeds, nuts, lentils, asparagus, pepper, cabbage

Nutrients	Benefits	Food sources
Vitamin B12 (Cyanocobalamin)	Helps blood carry oxygen. Uses protein for energy and DNA synthesis, Essential for nerves. Deals with tobacco smoke and other toxins	Oysters, sardines, tuna, lamb, eggs, shrimp, cottage cheese, milk, chicken, turkey, cheese
Folic Acid	Helps brain and nerve function. Utilises protein and helps in red cell formation. Very useful in pregnancy for baby's brain and nerve development	Wheat germ, spinach, sprouts, peanuts, hazelnuts, walnuts, sesame seeds, cauliflower, cashew nuts, avocado, broccoli, asparagus
Biotin	Helps the body to use fat. Promotes healthy skin, hair, and nerves	Lettuce, cauliflower, peas, tomato, oysters, grapefruit, watermelon, sweet corn, almonds, cherries, milk, eggs, cabbage
Vitamin C (Ascorbic Acid)	Strengthens the immune system to fight against infections. Produces collagen. Keeps bones, skin, and joints firm. Builds anti-stress hormones. Turns food into energy	Peppers, watercress, cabbage, broccoli, kiwi, melon, orange, grapefruit, lime, lemon, cauliflower, strawberries, tomato
Vitamin D	Maintains strong healthy bones and teeth by retaining calcium. Supports nervous system's health. Regulates insulin levels. Helps lung function and cardiovascular health. Influences the expression of genes involved in cancer development	Mackerel, herring, salmon, cottage cheese, oysters, eggs

Nutrients	Benefits	Food sources
Vitamin E (d-alpha Tocopherol)	Antioxidant, very good for skin. Protects cells from damage and against cancer. Helps body use oxygen. Prevents blood clots. Improves wound healing	Unrefined cold-pressed corn oils, sunflower seeds, peanuts, sesame seeds, beans, peas, tuna, salmon, sweet potato
Vitamin K (Phylloquinone)	Prevents ear disease. Bone health. Reduces neural damage. Reduces postoperative bruising. Neutralises free radicals	Cauliflower, lettuce, cabbage, beans, broccoli, asparagus, corn oil, milk, tomato, Brussels sprout
Bioflavonoids	Help vitamin C work. Strengthen capillaries. Speed up wound healing and muscle injuries. Antioxidant and DNA protector	Berries, cherries, citrus fruits
Choline	Helps break fat in the liver. Protects the lungs. Facilitates movement of fats into cells and synthesis in the nervous system	Lecithin, eggs, fish, liver, soya beans, peanuts, whole grain, nuts, citrus, brewer's yeast, wheat germ
Coenzyme Q10	Energy metabolism. Improves heart function. Normalises blood pressure. Increases exercise tolerance. Antioxidant. Boosts immunity system	Sardines, mackerel, spinach, soya oil, peanuts, sesame seeds, walnuts
Inositol	Needed for cell growth. Mild tranquiliser. Maintains healthy hair. Helps you relax and sleep better. Decreases blood cholesterol	Lecithin, granules, soy flour, eggs, fish, liver, citrus fruits, nuts, melon, brewer's yeast

Nutrients Promoters and Adversaries

- Promoters are factors that assist absorption or utilisation of each nutrient.
- Adversaries are factors that hinder absorption or utilisation of each nutrient.

Nutrients	Promoters	Adversaries
Vitamin A (Retinol and Beta-Carotene)	Zinc Vitamins C and E	Heat, light, alcohol, coffee, smoking
Vitamin B1 (Thiamine)	B complex vitamins Magnesium Manganese	Antibiotics, tea, processed foods, coffee, stress, birth control pill, alkaline agents, baking powder, sulfur dioxide, overcooked foods
Vitamin B2 (Riboflavin)	B complex vitamins and Selenium Best taken with food	Alcohol, birth control pills, tea, coffee, alkaline agents, overcooked foods, and food refining
Vitamin B3 (Niacin)	B complex vitamins and Chromium Best taken with food	Antibiotics, tea, coffee, birth control pills, alcohol
Vitamin B5 (Pantothenic acid)	B complex vitamins Biotin Folic acid Best taken with food	Stress, alcohol, tea, coffee. Destroyed by heat and processed food
Vitamin B6 (Pyridoxine)	B complex vitamins Magnesium Zinc	Alcohol, smoking, birth control pills, protein, processed and refined food
Vitamin B12 (Cyanocobalamin)	B complex vitamins Folic acid Best taken with food	Alcohol, smoking, lack of stomach acid, stress

Nutrients	Promoters	Adversaries
Folic Acid	B complex vitamins especially B12 to be taken with food	High temperature, light, processed food, birth control pills
Biotin	B complex vitamin Magnesium Manganese	Raw egg white and fried food
Vitamin C (Ascorbic Acid)	Bioflavonoids in fruits and vegetables increase its effect with B complex vitamins to produce energy Vitamin E	Smoking, alcohol, pollution, stress, fried foods
Vitamin D	Exposure to sunlight, Vitamin D being made in the skin Vitamins A, C, and E protect vitamin D	Lack of sunlight, fried foods
Vitamin E (d-alpha Tocopherol)	Works with vitamin C and Selenium	High-temperature cooking especially frying, birth control pills, excessive intake of refined and processed fats and oils
Vitamin K (Phylloquinone)	Healthy intestinal bacteria; there is no need for dietary source	Antibiotics
Bioflavonoids	Vitamin C	Free radicals, stress, processed foods
Choline	-	-
Coenzyme Q10	-	-
Inositol	-	-

Minerals and their benefits

Nutrients	Benefits	Food sources
Calcium	Promotes healthy heart and nerves. Reduces menstrual cramps. Relieves tremors, aching muscles and bones. Improves teeth health and skin. Maintains acid-alkaline balance	Swiss cheese, cheddar cheese, almonds, parsley, artichoke, prunes, cooked dried beans, brewer's yeast
Chromium	Balances blood sugar. Helps normalise hunger and cravings. Improves teeth life span. Protects DNA. Essential for heart function	Brewer's yeast, wholemeal bread, rye bread, oysters, potato, chicken, butter, Swiss cheese, lamb, eggs, green peppers, apple
Iron	Transports oxygen and carbon dioxide (CO_2) to and from the cells. Component of enzymes. Vital for energy production	Pumpkin seeds, parsley, almonds, prunes, cashew nuts, raisins, pork, sesame seeds, pecan nuts, walnuts, dates
Magnesium	Strengthens bones and teeth. Promotes healthy muscles and helps them relax. Important for premenstrual symptoms relief. Essential for energy	Almonds, cashew nuts, brewer's yeast, garlic, peas, potato skin, crab, raisins, buckwheat flour
Manganese	Helps to form healthy bones and cartilage tissues nerves. Activates 20 enzymes. Stabilises sugar in the blood. Promotes healthy DNA	Watercress, pineapple, okra, endive, blackberries, raspberries, lettuce, oats, strawberries, beetroot, celery, lima beans
Molybdenum	Gets rid of uric acid. Strengthens teeth. Reduces caries in teeth. Detoxifies the body from free radicals. Produces insulin. Reduces cell damage and is required for brain function	Tomato, wheat germ, pork, lamb, lentils, beans
Phosphorus	Forms and maintains bones and teeth. Needed for milk secretion. Builds muscle tissue. Produces energy. Component of DNA	Present in almost all foods

Nutrients	Benefits	Food sources
Potassium	Enables nutrients to move into cells and waste products to move out of cells. Promotes healthy nerves and muscles. Maintains fluid balance in the body. Relaxes muscles. Helps secretion of insulin for blood sugar. Stimulates gut movements	Watercress, endive, cabbage, celery, parsley, zucchini, radishes, cauliflower, mushrooms, pumpkin, banana, molasses
Selenium	Antioxidant that protects against free radicals and carcinogens. Reduces inflammation. Stimulates immune system. Boosts men's fertility	Tuna, oysters, molasses, mushrooms, herrings, cottage cheese, cabbage, beef liver, zucchini, cod, chicken
Sodium	Maintains body water balance. Prevents dehydration. Helps nerve functioning. Produces energy	Olives, beetroot, cabbage, cottage cheese, red kidney beans, watercress, crab, miso, shrimps, sauerkraut
Zinc	Component of 200 enzymes in the body and DNA. Essential for growth. Important for healing. Controls hormones. Helps cope with stress. Good for bones, teeth, and hair	Oysters, ginger root, lamb, pecan nuts, haddock, peas, shrimps, turnips, egg yolks, whole wheat grain, rye, oats, almonds

Minerals Promoters and Adversaries

Nutrients	Promoters	Adversaries
Calcium	Normalises hunger. Reduces cravings	Excessive cold sweat, dizziness, irritability after six hours without food, needs frequent meals, cold hands, excessive thirst, addiction to sweets
Chromium	Vitamin B3 and 3 amino acids: glycine, glutamine, and cysteine combine to form glucose tolerance factor. Improved diet and exercise	High intake of refined sugar and flours. Excess body fat, additives, pesticides, petroleum products, processed foods, toxic metals
Iron	Vitamin C increases iron absorption. Vitamin E Calcium Folic acid Stomach acid Phosphorus	Oxalates (all bran flakes), rhubarb, tannic acid tea, wheat bran, phosphates (soft drinks, food additives), increased zinc and calcium intake
Magnesium	Vitamins B1, B6, C, D Zinc Calcium Phosphorus	Large amounts of calcium in dairy, proteins, fats, oxalates (all bran), wheat, bread
Manganese	Zinc Vitamins E, B1, C, K	Antibiotics, alcohol, refined foods, calcium, phosphorus
Molybdenum	Protein including Sulfur amino acids Carbohydrates Fats	Copper Sulfates

Nutrients	Promoters	Adversaries
Phosphorus	Correct calcium phosphorus ratio Lactose Vitamin D	Too much Iron, Magnesium, Aluminium
Potassium	Magnesium helps hold Potassium in cells	Excess Sodium from salt, alcohol, sugar, diuretics, laxatives, corticosteroid drug, stress
Selenium	Vitamins E, A, and C	Refined foods, modern farming techniques
Sodium	Vitamin D	Potassium, Chloride counteracts Sodium to keep the body in the body
Zinc	Stomach acids Vitamins A, E, B6 Magnesium Calcium Phosphorus	Wheat, oxalates (all bran flakes), high Calcium intake, Copper, low protein intake, excess sugar intake, stress. Alcohol prevents uptake

Essential Oils and their benefits

Nutrients	Benefits	Food sources
Omega 3	Healthy heart. Thins blood. Reduces inflammation. Improves nervous system functioning. Promotes neurotransmitters. Relieves depression. Helps in attention deficit, hyperactivity and autism. Improves sleep and skin. Helps balance hormones	Mackerel, swordfish, marlin, tuna, salmon, sardines, flax seeds, sunflower seeds
Omega 6	Healthy heart. Thins blood. Reduces inflammation. Improves nervous system functioning. Promotes neurotransmitters	Safflower oil, sunflower oil, walnuts, sesame seeds, wheat germ

Essential Oils Promoters and Adversaries

Nutrients	Promoters	Adversaries
Omega 3	Niacin Vitamins B6, C Zinc Magnesium Manganese Antioxidants nutrients protect them	Frying, food storage, food processing (hydrogenation), smoking, alcohol
Omega 6	Omega 3 Niacin Vitamins B6, C Zinc Magnesium Manganese Antioxidants nutrients protect them	Frying, food storage, food processing (hydrogenation), smoking, alcohol

Fibre: The Zero-Calorie Carbohydrate

Fibre is an indigestible cell wall component of plant foods. It includes waxes, lignin, and polysaccharides such as cellulose and pectin. Unlike starches and sugars, which are other types of carbohydrates, when we consume fibre, we add bulk to food, but get zero calories from it and no food energy. It comes from fruits, vegetables, grains, nuts, and legumes. It is not broken down and absorbed in the bloodstream, but passes through the entire digestive tract.

Soluble and Insoluble Fibres

Soluble fibre: Dissolves in water, it helps lower blood cholesterol and glucose levels. Found in oats, peas, beans, apples, citrus fruits, carrots, barley, etc.

Insoluble fibre: Doesn't dissolve in water, it promotes the movement of material through your digestive system and increases stool bulk. It is helpful for people who struggle with constipation and irregular stool. Found in whole wheat flour, wheat bran, nuts, beans, and vegetables such as cauliflower, green beans, potatoes, cabbage, onions, dark leafy vegetables, raisins, root vegetable skins, cucumbers, zucchini, brown rice, bulgur, couscous, barley, etc.

In the average diet: Three-fourth of the fibre is insoluble and one-fourth is soluble. We tend to eat a lot of bread and grain-based foods, but not enough fruits and vegetables. Excess of fibre could lead to cramps and bloating. A fibre deficiency in your diet can cause irregular digestion, elevated cholesterol levels, and increased body weight. A lack of fibre intake can cause constipation. Drink plenty of water and fluids. Many fibre-rich foods provide a good source of antioxidants and bind with harmful toxins, excorting them out of your body.

Serving large portions of chunky vegetable soup at the start of the meal increases satiety and reduces the total amount of calories you eat by 20 per cent. Having salads or whole fruits (particularly apples and pears) before a meal reduces the number of calories you eat by 15 per cent. High-fibre and high-water foods, reduce your appetite, and cause you to eat smaller amounts of the higher calorie foods.

Juicing as opposed to blending removes the fibre. The polyphenols bound to fibre within the plant cell may not make it to the colon. The beneficial antioxidants are available via blending the fruits or vegetables, or eating them whole rather than juicing.

Make sure to include "top foods" containing the above nutrients in your shopping list, and if you have any deficiency, take the recommended daily requirements as prescribed by your general practitioner.

It's also wise to have probiotics (beneficial bacteria) to balance bacteria for a healthy digestion and keep your immune system strong to fight infections. Good bacteria, known as Lactobacillus and Bifidobacteria, keep bad bacteria under control. You may find them in fermented foods such as yoghurt, or cottage cheese, or as supplements. Daily intake promotes healthy intestinal flora, prevents disease and stress. Prebiotics, found in bananas, barley, garlic, Jerusalem artichoke, onions, soya beans, and wheat, are another way to boost the healthy gut bacteria.

Medical science considers the presence of any of the diseases listed below as a sign of probable antioxidant deficiency:

- Alzheimer's
- Cancer
- Heart disease
- Diabetes
- Hypertension
- Rheumatoid arthritis
- Mental illness
- Cataracts
- Respiratory tract infections.

Vegetables, legumes, herbs, spices, and fruits are excellent sources of important cancer-fighting and anti ageing phytonutrients as well as antioxidants. To get the full spectrum of phytonutrients and antioxidants, you need to eat a wide variety of natural foods from every colour of the rainbow. They talk directly to your genes, altering genetic expression and silencing oncogenes (cancer-causing genes); moreover they increase the expression of cancer suppressor genes.

Oxygen is the basis of life, yet it is chemically reactive and can become unstable and capable of oxidising neighbouring molecules. This can lead to cellular damage that triggers cancer, inflammation, arterial damage, and ageing. Free oxidising radicals are the bodily equivalent of nuclear waste and must be disarmed to remove the danger. Free radicals are made in all combustion processes, including smoking, the burning of petrol to create exhaust fumes, radiation, frying, barbecuing food, and normal body processes, such as breathing, moving, and digestion.

Chemicals capable of disarming free radicals are called antioxidants. The balance between our antioxidants intake and our exposure to free radicals may be the balance between life and death. Some antioxidants are essential nutrients needed for survival, such as vitamins A, C, and E.

The best results in ageing studies show that a low-calorie diet high in antioxidant nutrients reduces oxidative stress and ensures maximum antioxidant protection. The best antioxidant combination includes vitamins E and C, Beta-Carotene, Glutathione, Anthocyanidins, Lipoic acid, and Coenzyme Q10. Taking one of these on its own, in wrong doses or combinations, can do more harm than good. You need to get a correct nutrient dosage from your doctor as it varies from one individual to another. Meanwhile, you can enrich your intake by eating proper antioxidant foods.

Best Antioxidant Foods

These are berries, grapes, tomatoes, mustard, broccoli, and herbs such as turmeric. Beta-carotene is found in red, orange, yellow vegetables, and fruits.

Vitamin C is abundant in vegetables and fruits eaten raw (attention: heat destroys it).

Vitamin E is found in seed foods like nuts, seeds, and their oils, vegetables like peas, broad beans, corn, and whole grains.

Vitamin A is found in sweet potatoes, carrots, watercress, peas, and broccoli provided you do not fry them.

Based on the Tufts University Boston research, there's a new way to rate a food's overall antioxidant power. Each food will be assigned a certain number of ORAC units (Oxygen Radical Absorbance Capacity), which ranks the ability of the antioxidant food compound to absorb free radicals. Foods that score high in these units are especially helpful in countering oxidant, or free radicals' damage in your body. Top scoring foods according to the ORAC classification include prunes, raisins, blueberries, blackberries, kale, spinach, strawberries, raspberries, plums, broccoli, and alfalfa sprouts. You need to eat them every day to stay young and energetic.

ORAC rankings

Per 100 grams	ORAC units	Per item or serving	ORAC units
Blueberries	2234	½ cup	1620
Blackberries	2036	½ cup	1466
Tenderstem broccoli	1183	½ cup cooked	1159
Kale	1770	½ cup cooked	1150
Strawberries	1536	½ cup	1144
Spinach steamed	909	½ cup cooked	1089
Raisins	2830	¼ cup	1019
Broccoli	888	½ cup cooked	817
Raspberries	1227	½ cup	755
Beets: beetroot	841	½ cup cooked, sliced	715
Spinach raw	1210	1 cup raw	678
Plums	949	1 plum	626
Prunes	5770	1 pitted prune	462
Alfalfa sprouts	931	1 cup	307
Avocado	782	½ cup	149

Note that boiling can reduce ORAC values by up to 90 per cent, while steaming retains more of the antioxidants.

Phytochemicals

Phytochemicals are biologically active compounds in food. They are not classified as essential nutrients, in that our lives do not depend on them as they do on vitamins. However, they play a vital role in the body's biochemistry in ways that affect our health as significantly as vitamins and minerals. They are referred to as "nature's pharmacy." They directly influence our gene expression. For example, "resveratrol" (a polyphenol type present in grapes and cocoa powder) activates longevity genes. "Anthocyanins" (a class of flavonoid) and berry components are potent agents protective of our DNA and genomic activity.

Fruits and vegetables, apart from being good sources of vitamins, minerals, and fibre, are also rich sources of phytochemicals. They are not stored in the body; therefore it is best to eat foods rich in phytochemicals on a regular basis.

Top 30 Phytochemicals with proven health benefits

Allium compounds: garlic, onions, leeks **Benefits:** protect against stomach cancer, lower cholesterol, and prevent atherosclerosis (disease in which plaque builds up in your arteries resulting in a risk of hypertension and diabetes). Help prevent blood clots	**Anthocyanidins**: grapes and berries. Dried berries and grapes contain high concentration **Benefits:** against gout and certain types of arthritis	**Bioflavonoids**: berries, broccoli, buckwheat (includes rutin), tomatoes, wine, citrus fruits (includes hesperidin), rosehips, cherries, grapes, papaya, cantaloupe melon, plums, tea, cucumbers **Benefits:** potent antioxidants binding to toxic metals and escorting them out of the body. Stabilise vitamin, have a bacteriostatic and antibiotic effect, are anticarcinogenic. Strengthen capillaries, speed up healing of wounds
Boswellic acid: herb frankincense **Benefits:** anti-inflammatory agent, produces the death of cancer cells (in particular brain tumours, leukaemia, and colon cancer), helpful with arthritis, decreases asthma symptoms	**Capsaicin:** chilli, hot pepper **Benefits:** protects DNA from damage, anticancer (prostate and lung in particular*), analgesic to treat postsurgical and osteoarthritic pain, reduces pain from rheumatoid arthritis, joint or muscle pain from fibromyalgia. Capsaicin supplements help in weight loss (decrease appetite, increase satiety, and decrease food intake)	**Carotenoids:** carrots, sweet potato, tomatoes cooked for 30 minutes, peas, sweet potato, watercress **Benefits:** antiageing antioxidants, prevent heart disease and heart attack by inhibiting the formation of LDL cholesterol, combat free radicals. Beta-carotene increases when carrots are cooked

THE SECOND STEP

Chlorophyll: green vegetables, seaweed, algae **Benefits:** helps protect against cancer, powerful wound healer, and helps build the blood (together with vitamins C, B12, B6, A, K, and folic acid)	**Chlorogenic acid:** pineapple, tomato, green pepper, carrot, strawberry **Benefits:** prevents the formation of cancer-causing nitrosamines	**Coumarins:** cinnamon, apricot, liquorice, strawberry, cherry, cherry, sweet clover, green peppers, pineapple, carrot, tomato **Benefits:** prevent the formation of cancer-causing nitrosamines, anti-fungicidal, not to be taken with anticoagulants
Curcumin: turmeric, curry, mustard, corn, yellow pepper **Benefits:** treats wounds, skin conditions, digestive problems, ability to kill cancers (breast, colon, prostate, and skin), improves digestion, anti-inflammatory, powerful antioxidant	**Dithiolthiones:** Cruciferous vegetables: kale, cauliflower, cabbage, broccoli and Brussels sprouts **Benefits:** cancer prevention	**Ellagic acid:** strawberries, grapes, raspberries **Benefits:** neutralises carcinogens before they damage DNA. It puts off the action of nitrosamine, a cancer-producing chemical found in some meat. Protects from aflatoxin (a carcinogen found in peanuts). Second to garlic for its anticancer properties. High antioxidant levels
Genistein: soya beans, tofu, soya milk **Benefits:** prevents cancer (breast, prostate) and prevents lumps from growing and spreading	**Glucosinolates:** broccoli, Brussels sprouts, cruciferous vegetables, Tenderstem broccoli, strawberries, raspberries. **Benefits:** detoxify the liver, reduce the risk for lung and stomach cancer*	**Indoles:** cabbage, kale, mustard, radish, cruciferous vegetables, Brussels sprouts, cauliflower, horseradish, kale, mustard, turnips **Benefits:** lower incidence of colon cancer

Isothiocyanates (ICT): turnips, strawberries, raspberries, cabbage, kale, mustard, radish, cruciferous vegetables, Brussels sprouts, cauliflower, horseradish, mustard **Benefits**: lower incidence of colon cancer	**Lignans**: beans, nuts, flax seeds, sesame **Benefits**: mimic the actions of endogenous estrogens
Lentinan: mushrooms, shiitake, reishi. **Benefits**: widely used in Japanese hospitals to treat cancer. Induces the production of interferon, the body's own antiviral chemical used to fight off infection	**Phenols and Polyphenols**: green tea, berries **Benefits**: potent antioxidants. Have cancer protective effects, more powerful than those in vitamins C and E. In Japan, 3 cups of green tea are consumed a day, partly responsible for low levels of cancer found in the country. Raspberry ketones, a form of polyphenol, may aid weight loss
Lutein: cabbage, spinach, broccoli, cauliflower, kale **Benefits**: powerful antioxidant. Heat-stable and can survive cooking. Protects the eyes	**Lycopene**: tomato juice, mashed and cooked, watermelon, red foods **Benefits**: powerful antioxidant. Anticancer properties found in tomatoes
Phytoestrogens: sweet fennel or liquorice tea, fennel, soya, tofu, miso, celery, wheat, liquorice, citrus fruits, alfalfa **Benefits**: bind excess of oestrogens made in the body to a protein made in the blood. A high intake of phytoestrogens is associated with a low risk for breast and prostate cancer, menopausal symptoms, fibroids, and other hormone-related diseases	**Phytosterols**: vegetable oils, seeds, beans, lentils, seeds oils. **Benefits**: lower plasma total and LDL cholesterol (low-density lipoprotein) by absorbing it from the small intestine
	Piperine: only in black pepper **Benefits**: helps absorb more nutrients from your food

Proanthocyanidins: berries, grapes, dried and fresh beans, chickpeas **Benefits**: treat androgenic alopecia (hair loss) and act as a modulator of the immune response	**Probiotics:** fermented foods such as yoghurt, or cottage cheese, or as supplements **Prebiotics** found in bananas, barley, garlic, Jerusalem artichoke, onions, soy beans, and wheat; they are another way to boost the healthy gut bacteria **Benefits**: balance bacteria for a healthy digestion, keep your immune system strong to fight infections, promote healthy intestinal flora, and prevent disease and stress	**Quercetin** (kind of bioflavonoid): strawberries, berries **Benefits**: improves capillaries' health and connective tissues. Alleviates bruising, oedema, varicose veins. Inhibits the release of histamine. Acts as a neurotransmitter for the brain, spinal cord, and uterus. Helps reduce eczema, asthma, hay fever, and has anti-inflammatory properties. Mayo Clinic in the United States researched how quercetin blocks prostate cancer cells growth
Saponins: peanuts, quinoa, soya, tomato **Benefits**: decrease blood lipids. Lower cancer risks. Lower blood glucose response.	**Sulforaphane**: broccoli, cauliflower, kale, turnips, Brussels sprouts, tenderstem **Benefits**: natural antibacterial compound. Reduces risk of stomach cancer and ulcers (kills off the Helicobacter)	**Zeaxanthin**: spinach, peas, cabbage, broccoli, corn **Benefits**: protects against age-related eye diseases such as cataracts

*American Association for Cancer Research; World Cancer Research Fund, Japanese Hospitals, Mayo Clinic (United States).

It takes time for the effects of dietary changes to manifest in the mind. Changing your diet may not impact your psychology overnight, but in months it can affect it significantly. Nutrition is a way of living. You could check with your doctor if you have any deficiency in your essential vitamins and minerals, through a blood test.

Eat healthily, eat regularly, have small portions in the day (five times), and choose what food is good for you. It is all a matter of balancing quantity and quality.

Movement

I wrote movement on purpose rather than exercise as personally, I suffered from consistency when I used the word exercise. I would be super motivated as I "should" exercise then two weeks later I would drop. Replacing with the word movement to awaken my body and mind after long hours of motionless, made a huge difference in my results, in addition to my consistency. Try it. Think of the importance of movement for your mental and physical health. Enjoy the process and don't be obsessed by its necessity.

The Centres for Disease Control and Prevention encourage most adults to get at least 150 minutes of moderate-intensity aerobic activity per week. You can reach this goal by taking a brisk thirty-minute walk around your neighbourhood, five days a week.

Physical activity as highlighted by the World Health Organisation (WHO) for adults aged between eighteen to sixty-four years includes: walking, dancing, gardening, hiking, swimming, cycling, household chores, sports.

- Aerobic high cardio activity at least for ten minutes, followed by thirty minutes of moderate-intensity activity, five times per week.
- Muscle-strengthening activities involving your major muscle groups, to be done twice a week.

These recommendations are relevant to all healthy adults unless specific medical conditions indicate the contrary.

Ten Benefits of Physical Activity:

1. Improve your memory and brain function.
2. Protect against many chronic diseases.
3. Aid in weight management.
4. Lower blood pressure and improve heart health.
5. Improve your quality of sleep.
6. Reduce feelings of anxiety and depression. People's moods significantly improve after engaging in exercise (University of Bristol Study, 2008).
7. Lower rates of all-cause mortality.
8. Improve joint pain and stiffness.
9. Maintain muscle strength and balance.
10. Increase life span, fitness level, and muscular composition.

Assessment level

Adapt the fitness programme to fit you. Get an evaluation based on your body needs, mass, and muscle composition. You can choose from a beginner, moderate, or advanced programme depending on your fitness level.

There are many indoors and outdoors fitness activities you could choose from:

- Cardio like running, cycling, body combat, kickboxing.
- Dancing like zumba, oriental...
- Yoga and pilates.
- Aerobic circuit training combining muscular resistance and strength building. Get lean, toned, and fit doing a total body workout using light to moderate weights with repetition...

To kick off and create a fitness habit, start with a personal trainer who will customise a programme based on your needs and goals, as well as your physical and health history. He/she will motivate you and correct you while exercising to avoid any injury. You will notice results after a month if you practice thrice a week.

Sleep

- Are you struggling with your sleep?
- Are you experiencing low-quality sleep?
- Do you wake up in the middle of the night or in the morning feeling tired?
- Do you awake feeling as if you ran a marathon during your sleep, or as though you fell off a cliff?
- Do you have weird dreams or nightmares?

Throughout my journey, I noticed that the quality of my sleep depended on many factors:

- What I did before going to bed.
- What I ate in the evening.
- What I thought of.

- What I went through during my day.
- What I watched on television or on my phone.

No matter how many hours I slept, the quality of my sleep and the way I woke-up depended on how well I slept. I made it a routine to go to bed before 10:30 p.m. and wake up by 7:00 a.m.

- I eat light meals, avoid red meat for diner, as I noticed I was agitated and restless at night.
- I stop all screens an hour before going to bed.
- I prepare my room, my bed environment, removing all distractions and possible noises.
- I usually listen to soft music, make sure no light filters in.
- I relax in the bed, meditate, pray, calm my inner thoughts and drink Chamomile before sleeping.
- I regulate my room temperature and switch on the air purifier.
- During the night, my phone is not welcome, I put it on aeroplane mode and away from me.
- I don't have a television in the room to avoid being invaded by its content.
- When I have a hectic day, I take a bath, with candle lights, soft music and just unwind. Me time! I just love it.
- I noticed as well that any exciting activity I did after 10 P.M., would jeopardise my sleep and would intensify my dreams. My energy depended on my sleep. I feel inefficient, sleepy, and very irritable if I had a bad sleep.

As per the World Sleep Society, the ten tips for better sleep are:

1. Establish a regular bedtime and waking time.
2. Allow yourself to take a nap if you feel tired (I take a power nap whenever I feel the need).
3. Adjust to a healthier lifestyle regarding alcohol and food intake.

4. Create a caffeine cut-off time (I do not exceed three coffees per day and my last one is after lunch).
5. Change your bedtime snack to a calming treat.
6. Watch your workout routine (for me exercising in the evening causes sleep disruption. I am more productive and energised when I exercise in the morning).
7. Use comfortable inviting bedding (I change my mattress every seven years and pillows every year. I also make sure my bed invites me to dip-in).
8. Find a comfortable sleep temperature setting and ensure your room is well ventilated.
9. Block-out all distracting noise and eliminate light as much as possible.
10. Reserve your bed for sleep, sex, and not for work or general recreation.

While sleep requirements vary from person to person, the World Health Organisation (WHO) recommends seven to nine hours of sleep per night for adults to function at their best.

My advice is to listen to your body and get to know what works best for you, we are so different. Take care of your sleep, it is key to your performance and mood, to stay mentally, emotionally, and physically healthy.

"Prioritise quality sleep, it's the best meditation."

Oprah Winfrey

"Your future depends on your dreams. So go to SLEEP."

Mezut Barazany

The Third Step

Design your Future

Architect your roadmap with meaningful goals

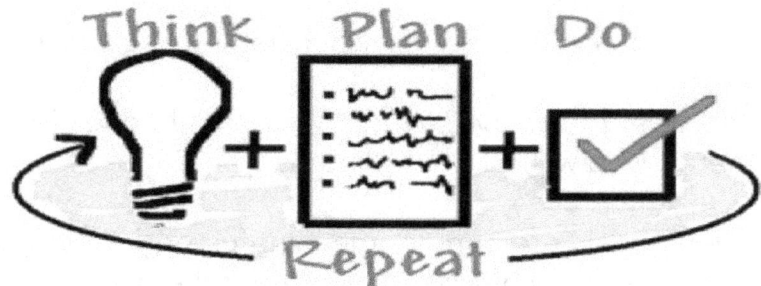

Source: yourtherapysource.com

S.M.A.R.T.E.R Goal-Setting Technique

Specific
Measurable
Achievable
Relevant
Timeable
Enjoyable
Reviewable

I added " ER " on the known SMART goal-setting technique to reflect on the importance of continuous evaluation and feedback. Monitor your progress regularly, if you are on track, review any discrepancies to ensure you achieve your goal. Act **PASSIONATELY** (heart and mind working hand in hand) and **ENJOY** each step of the way.

"It should scare you a little and excite you a lot."

Joe Vitale

The gap between where you are and where you want to be, is how much clarity, focus, energy, effort, time, and commitment you put into your goal to fulfill you.

Specific
Answer each of these questions when setting your goals.

What do I want to achieve? Why? Where am I now? How can I reach there? Who will do what? And by when?

Ensure your goals are simple, meaningful, and very specific, which will help you achieve them, and get the necessary inner and outer resources.

Example: "I am happy, I handle every unhelpful emotion by learning from it and letting it go."

Measurable
A measurable goal tells you when you have accomplished it. In the above example, you can track **daily** your results to find out how you are progressing towards reaching your goal. How will you know you have achieved it from a sensory acuity point of view? What would you need to see, hear, smell, taste, touch, feel? And say to yourself? What should happen for you to know you achieved it? What proof or evidence do you have?

"I am happy, I handle every unhelpful emotion by learning from it and letting it go. I am focused. My mind is clear. I feel great. My face radiates with happiness and faith. I hear my laughs. I am calm inside."

Achievable as of now, **with the end in mind**
Write your goal with the end in mind, stated in the **present** tense and in positive words (look at the words in the previous examples). "What specifically do you want to achieve NOW?" It will give direct orders to your unconscious mind to find the resources. If you use the future tense (I will be happy...), the message to your mind will be, "We have time." Or "I don't want to suffer," what you will end up doing is suffering.

Do set high goals, plan them through several steps to avoid losing motivation, and giving up after a while. Be stubborn and flexible in your approaches, and keep going till you reach them. You have zero excuses.

Relevant
Have multiple goals planned, that is, short, medium, and long term. They should contribute to achieving your overall purpose, and make sure they are aligned with your values. Set reasonable, realistic, resourced, and result-based goals.

Timeable
Every goal you set must be dated and time-limited.

Enjoyable
Whatever your goal is, have fun, be fully excited, and engaged while doing it. Let all your senses vibrate with exhilaration.

Reviewable
Managing goal setting is similar to managing your diary. You need to have follow-up dates (daily, weekly, end of the month, beginning of the month, etc.) even though you have a target date. This will allow you to measure attainability by evaluating your progress and rectifying the goal and target date. This will avoid frustration, you renouncing, and setting yourself up for failure.

Base your decision on:
- Does your goal align with your values and belief?
- Does it fulfill your innermost callings, what you are missing in your being, having or doing?
- Will it move you closer to your purpose and vision?

GROW Model

GROW stands for:
Goal
Reality
Options (or Obstacles)
What Next (or Way Forward).

Sir John Whitmore

Some additional questions to plan your strategy

- What problems *specifically* do you want to solve?
- What changes do you want to make to improve your results?
- What do you have that you are not using?
- What resources do you need?
- What are you afraid of?
- What is not achieving your goal costing you?
- What must change for you to achieve this goal?
- What approaches have you seen other people use? Who might be able to help you? Who could you learn from? How does he or she do it? (physically, mentally, and technically)
- How will you get that support?

> **"Shoot for the moon.
> Even if you miss,
> You'll land among the stars."**
>
> Les Brown

"Change occurs at the unconscious level and creates long-lasting results.
Having a mission, vision, and goals determine your focus and therefore your results.
Outcomes are determined by your expectations.
Increase your behavioural flexibility in each situation to be more effective.
Choice is yours; design processes to gain more choices.
Enough people you help get what they want most; you will get what you want most."

Christopher Howard

"A goal without a plan is just a wish."

Antoine de Saint-Exupéry

"Put a deadline on your dream."

Harsha Bhogle

"The distance between dreams and reality is called **ACTION**."

Einstein

Your Roadmap to Happiness

Goals	Actions	Resources	People	Completion Date	Progress Monitoring Date	Measurement
What I want to achieve	**What** activities I need to do and **How**	**Which** and **where** can I find them	**Who** can help me	When	Follow up date	Achievement sensory proof (see, hear, smell, taste, feel, touch, self-talk)

The Book In One Page

- Love yourself: Embrace a healthy mind and body towards a HAPPY life.
- Focus your full attention on your innermost callings.
- Adopt my signature **Immune MNMS DETOX Formula**© (**M**ind, emotional, physical, and environmental detoxification, healthy **N**utrition, regular **M**ovement, and quality **S**leep).
- Build your resilience: Become aware - accept - forgive - heal - think - plan - do - REPEAT.
- Witness, observe, and surrender without any judgement, or imagination. Free yourself from the prison of your mind.
- Change what you're in control of, and accept what you can't change to RISE STRONGER.
- LET GO of your EGO. There is no failure and no giving up. There's only feedback and learning.
- Commit 100% with 0 excuses. Solution and opportunity oriented.
- LIVE in the present moment, completely focused on your senses' actual experience.
- Surround yourself with people who lift you higher, and participate in your growth.
- Be the architect of your destiny, the way you want it to be.
- Be the link to a world of unity and not separateness. Practice oneness with the Divine.
- Fix physical and emotional boundaries: What you will or won't accept.
- Open your eyes and look past the illusion, so that the truth can appear. YOU are HAPPINESS.
- Ask, believe, receive, and thank.
- Keep smiling, keep going, keep growing, you are doing GREAT!
- Be the HERO, not the victim.

Crash Wake-Up call

This book exists thanks to my car accident on Saturday, July 7, 2018, where I fell off a hill and ended up with my car in the river, upside down, with my seatbelt on.

Let me update you on what was going on in my life at that time. It was a very challenging period for me; we were facing a heavy financial crisis caused by my husband's employer, who failed to deliver on what he had committed in the contract and caused over two years of pure pain; there was difficulty in facing our financial engagements; fear of not making it; having to refuse our children's requests as it was really a matter of surviving, moreover, where you finally awake to who will stand by you in such a situation. There were many times when I felt hopeless, overwhelmed, and wanting to finish with it. Maybe it would have ended all the terrible situations surrounding us, and the craziest part is that you are not in control of any of it; you just need to cope.

I couldn't afford to go on holiday, but my husband insisted that I needed to take a break from all that is going on in our life at this stage. I accepted, unwillingly, to go to beautiful Italy, a country I look at as my second home.

What is really weird is that two weeks before I travelled, I had a nightmare, where I was literally falling off a mountain in my car. Is that a strange coincidence?

That Saturday night, I was sitting sadly in my garden. Roberta, my sister-in-law, called and asked me to join her for dinner to get away from my thoughts. I didn't feel like going out at all. I had this strange deep sensation with my inner voice binding me to the sofa. But I still went.

It was 11:00 p.m., and I was on a dark road in the mountain. I had to reverse the car to allow her to lead. Needless to say, she assisted the whole tragedy and rebirth.

I cannot describe all the thoughts that raced through in my head, the silence of the night mixed with the noise of the car compacting, the windows breaking, and my realisation that "I am going to die." I started praying, begging God to let me live. I hadn't seen Riccardo, my son, who lives in Switzerland. I didn't kiss goodnight Federico, my other son, and moreover I had left Alessandro, my husband in such a difficult moment. I could just hear myself invoking, "God, please save me." Meanwhile, I was trying to unlock my seatbelt and it wasn't unlocking. I could see the water rising, and my chances of getting out closing to null. All of a sudden, the seatbelt button clicked, and I saw myself with a superpower, getting out from the passenger seat through the half-broken window, without ripping myself, just little wounds, and I ended up face down on the grass, legs in the river, and then I lost consciousness.

I woke up to the screaming of Roberta checking if I was still alive. You bet I was. God gave me again another chance to live. He reminded me of what death looked like, what I will miss, and what I have to appreciate. I am definitely still needed on earth to pursue my mission, calling, and purpose.

I can never be grateful enough to God for his **UNCONDITIONAL** love and protection, daily support, and important presence in my life. I owe Him EVERYTHING, most of all, my new breath and this NEW BLESSED and fulfilling journey.

This is where *Happydemic* comes from. I started writing it following my accident recovery with another title, and with the purpose of spreading **as much FAITH and happiness as I possibly can.**

I just felt with this COVID-19 pandemic, in a time full of uncertainty, fear, and anxiety from a little invisible enemy, you could spread a pandemic of happiness instead. It is only through acceptance of what is, resilience, forgiveness, gratefulness, love, and compassion that we can see this through. It is necessary to bring back our ancestors values of a happy supportive and united community and certainly not live by intimidation, governed by fear or systems that enrich the models that we definitely do not want to take part in, nor resemble.

Take this moment as a pause in your life to think through and create a better now, today, and tomorrow, for you, for your children, and all those that are around you.

Wake up! It's NOW or never, direct your path towards Happiness and make the best out of your life. "If you love time, don't waste time, for time is what life is made up of," Bruce Lee. And as T. Harv Eker says: "How you do anything, you do everything."

Be *Happydemic*.

References

Books and Seminars

- Bandler and Grinder, *Introduction to NLP*
- Dr. Tad James, M.S., PhD., Time Line Therapy
- Christopher Howard, Turning Passions Into Profits
- Matthew Mc Kay, PhD, Jeffrey C. Wood PsyD; Jeffrey Brantley, MD, *Dialectical Behavioural Therapy*
- Sheri Van Dijk, MSW, *DBT made simple: A Step-by-Step Guide to Dialectical Behaviour Therapy*
- Eckhart Tolle, *The Power of Now*
- Tony Robbins, *The Giant Within*
- H.H. Sheikh Mohammed Bin Rashed Al Maktoum, *Reflections of Happiness and Positivity*
- Rhonda Byrne, *The Secret*
- Don Miguel Ruiz, *The Four Agreements*
- The Health Sciences Academy
- Linda Bonnar, *Press Play*
- Matt Avery, *Secrets of Happy People*

Websites

mataheri.com; sciencedirect.com; theworldcounts.com; my.happify.com; selfdeterminationtherapy.org; poisitivepsychologyprogramme.com; globalhealingcentre.com; lifepotential.ca; who.int; theayurvedaexperience.com; doctoroz.com; detoxdiy.com; planetayurveda.co.nz; revelian.com; takingcharge.csh.umn.edu; worldsleepsociety.org; simplypsychology.com; neurohealthchiro.com.au; mayoclinic.org; eagereyes.org;

Larissa Redaelli

More about the Author

Enjoying broad international exposure of over twenty-eight years, Swiss-Lebanese born, Larissa Redaelli started her career in hotels after obtaining a Hotel and Catering Management Diploma with honours from the Geneva Hotel Management School, Switzerland. She has over fourteen years of experience as Global Director of Sales and Marketing at several top hotel chains, and over fourteen years of expertise in Corporate Executive Leadership Consulting and Training for confidence-building and performance mastery, strategic visioning, producing talents, and building performant teams. In addition to leading and managing by example, revenue optimisation, and customer experience excellence.

Larissa is committed to helping leaders and organisations bridge setbacks for true success and manage change by nurturing a happiness mindset with her signature **"Immune MNMS DETOX Formula,"** a total workout. She touches your heart and impacts you for a lifetime. You will definitely be inspired to successfully DETOX inside-out, clear your mind and body, to focus on results and equilibrium for true happiness in life and at work. Those who have attended her seminars, workshops, talks and training sessions, emphasise the power she has to captivate her audience.

The training methodology she employs involves extensive personal and professional experiences, in addition to proven and tested best practices. Larissa has conducted various customised training programmes in Italy, Switzerland, Malta, Libya, Russia, Bahrain, and the United Arab Emirates.

Fluent in English, French, Arabic, and Italian, she has the ability to interface in all four languages.

Larissa is a qualified Performance Consultant and Master Results Coach with Advanced Neurological Repatterning, licensed by Christopher Howard Events in the United Kingdom; a licensed NLP Trainer by the American Board of NLP and Dr. Tad James, PhD; a Time Line Therapy Master Practitioner recognised by the Time Line Therapy Association; and a Master Practitioner in Hypnosis, certified by the American Board of Hypnosis; as well as a Nutritional Therapist by the Health Sciences Academy in the United Kingdom.

Larissa has been Professor and Consultant for EHG, Geneva Hotel Management School, and is at present their Alumni Ambassador in the Arabic Peninsula. Previously Professor and Consultant for SWISSAM, Hospitality Business School in St Petersburg and for HTMI, Hospitality and Tourism Management Institute Switzerland in Dubai.

Larissa is also the author of the best-selling know-how book, *Le Savoir-Vendre* (2012) for the hospitality and service industries. Le Savoir-Vendre is a complete interactive manual that gives the reader all the keys to success in serving customised selling strategies based on a mind-to-mind rapport built on care and openness.

Since 2013, Larissa has been living in the United Arab Emirates. Her inspiration for *Happydemic*, her second interactive book, where she delivers talks, consultancy and training solutions for various individuals and organisations. **PASSIONATE**, compassionate, customer-centric, super positive, humble, caring, full of drive and enthusiasm are some of the values that represent her.

MORE ABOUT THE AUTHOR

When you see a **smiley face**, you instantly think of **Larissa**.

Visit larissaredaelli.com for more information about her or connect with her, directly at contact@larissaredaelli.com

Introduction to Le Savoir-Vendre

Whether you are selling a product, a service or an idea, all sales know-how is based on a common starting step: knowing how to sell yourself, communicating and actively listening to succeed. With over 200 pages of invaluable information, Le Savoir-Vendre reveals strategic selling techniques based on serving customers with a salesperson profile that portrays the physiology and psychology of excellence. It allows the reader to gain more confidence in selling, presenting with impact and managing customer experiences. This interactive book includes all the keys to success in the seven steps' sales process, such as discovering a customer's thinking strategy, buying motivation values, product beliefs and much more.

Backed by Larissa's authentic passion for sales and more than 26 years of international experience, this is a one-of-a-kind book that does what few others do – distills the entire art of selling into a single manual.

Originally unveiled at the Geneva Hotel Management School EHG, you can find this special edition book on sale at the Geneva Hotel Management School, Payot bookstores in Switzerland, and via this website larissaredaelli.com.

This book is currently available in French. English edition coming soon.

With my Happydemic Success Wishes

Thank you for having read my story and I hope you enjoyed the journey.

I trust you found plenty of valuable insights to begin your new story chapter now, and I would love to hear about it.

Remember that your fulfilment depends on how much passion, energy, effort, time, discipline, and commitment you put to honour your deepest callings.

If you want to keep the momentum, join me to continue your growth with amazing leaders from all over the world, who are committed to full mental, emotional, physical and environmental detox. Share your transformational experience and inspire others on their *Happydemic* journey to live fully, and make this world a better and healthier place.

Scan this QR Code and join our *Happydemic* community today.

www.ingramcontent.com/pod-product-compliance
Lightning Source LLC
Chambersburg PA
CBHW071601080526
44588CB00010B/984